Larry Huebner's
WHENING TENNIS

In Tennis, as in Life, TIMING is Everything

8/13/05
For the Chambliss
family — Thank you
for your wonderful
hospitality —
Larry Huebner

Note for Librarians: a cataloguing record for this
book that includes Dewey Classification and US
Library of Congress numbers is available from
the National Library of Canada. The complete
cataloguing record can be obtained from the
National Library's online database at:
www.nlc-bnc.ca/amicus/index-e.html
ISBN 1-4120-1172-8

Printed in Victoria, BC, Canada

TRAFFORD

**This book was published *on-demand* in
cooperation with Trafford Publishing.**
On-demand publishing is a unique process and
service of making a book available for retail sale
to the public taking advantage of on-demand
manufacturing and Internet marketing. **On-demand
publishing** includes promotions, retail sales,
manufacturing, order fulfilment, accounting and
collecting royalties on behalf of the author.

Suite 6E, 2333 Government St.,
Victoria, B.C. V8T 4P4, CANADA
Phone   250-383-6864
Toll-free   1-888-232-4444
Fax   250-383-6804
E-mail   sales@trafford.com
www.trafford.com/robots/03-1550.html

10   9   8   7   6   5   4   3   2

for GRETCHEN
my wife, my love, my coach and trainer

ACKNOWLEDGMENTS

Every author needs help – in so many ways. I am certainly no exception. Even my computer has helped me, thanks to Lou Feliz, a software designer friend. The concern and help one gets from friends is most appreciated and absolutely needed, especially for new authors.

Several years ago, an acquaintance, O.J. Woodward, encouraged me to start writing about Central California Tennis, which got me thinking about writing this book first. Then, another friend and author, Peter Burwash, showed me how to get started.

Once I did start, Gene Rose, a well read Fresno author, critiqued some of the original text and pointed me in the right direction. Then, Mike Murach a Fresno publisher, also kindly read my manuscript and offered some great help.

Barbara Kern, an author herself and former editor for Scribner and Sons, got her red pen out and corrected my incredibly numerous errors. All the members of my family were also editors of spelling, punctuation, grammar, as well as content. I really needed all of these people's help.

When I reached the point where I needed photographic help my daughter's friend, Michele Raitano came to the rescue.

My dear Eri Sato in Japan has also offered to help with potential marketing in her country. She has also put me in contact with a possible translator and publisher.

I got some vitally needed professional help from Nasreen McMullen, an artist and graphic designer. She really brought the project together with her expertise.

I'm indebted to Trafford Publishing for their help throughout the process. Special thanks to Jennifer Taylor of Trafford for being available as my personal advisor getting the book ready to publish.

Everyone mentioned has contributed generously to the completion of WHENING TENNIS. Also, there have been numerous others that gave me new ideas and helpful comments. My sincere thanks to all, I couldn't have done it without you!

CONTENTS

CONTENTS, *Con't*

FOREWORD
by PETER BURWASH

Larry Huebner is the best tennis coach I have known. He is also one of the nicest human beings one could meet.

When I arrived at the Fig Garden Swim & Racquet Club in the fall of 1968, I had no idea what a strong impact Larry would have on my life.

At the time I was a struggling young tennis professional trying to survive on the tour. In spite of being a very marginal player, Larry offered to help me out for free. And during the next seven years, Larry, his wife Gretchen and their three kids, Jim, John, and Karin became my second family. Whenever I had a break from the tour I would fly to Fresno.

In 1975 I formed a company of tennis professionals that manages tennis facilities globally. Up to the year 2001, we have taught over 3 million students. And, of those 3 million students, a good percentage was indirectly influenced by Larry Huebner.

I have interacted with a multitude of tennis teachers, professionals and coaches over the years, and there are very few who truly understand the game, and more importantly, understand how to teach it. Larry Huebner is in this elite class.

In life it is often not the marquis name who makes a difference, but rather those who toil humbly and diligently in relative obscurity within their profession.

When Larry talked to me about writing a book, I enthusiastically endorsed the idea.

One of the key ingredients of happiness in life is sharing. And I am honored to be able to write this foreword and encourage you to read on. Larry Huebner is sharing with you a bundle of gems so you can enjoy the sport by getting your game to another level.

Larry is one of the most sincere, dedicated individuals I have met. I thank him for all that he did for me as a role model on and off the court. It has been an honor to know him. You are now about to learn from one of tennis' truly great ambassadors.

Peter Burwash, Canadian Davis Cupper and Founder of Peter Burwash International.

INTRODUCTION TO
Whening Tennis
In Tennis, as in Life, TIMING is Everything

When I first thought of writing about my lifetime of tennis, the person I felt I needed to talk to was Peter Burwash, a former Canadian Davis Cup player I had coached. He was experienced in tennis coaching himself as head of PBI, the worldwide tennis teaching company he had founded. And most importantly to me, he was experienced as an instructional editor for Tennis Magazine and as a writer who was working on his tenth book.

I've had this idea that *when* you do something in tennis, as in life, it's often the most crucial part of the action. "When" kept coming into my mind as the focus for this book. But I needed some direction to get started. Peter has helped me with this and has been flattering as usual in his forward.

I have to tell you a little story about how his flattery set me straight a few years ago. It was in the 1994 Northern California Tennis Yearbook that Peter wrote an article titled "The Leading Edge" in which he outlined the top traits of twenty-five tennis "greats". He described Jimmy Conners as "enthusiastic", John McEnroe as "adaptable", Rod Laver as "secure", and among others, such as Michael Chang, Martina Navratilova, and Billie Jean King, he included me as "exemplar" and the coach he would take on tour. Now, I was indeed flattered by this accolade so I showed the article to my dear wife, Gretchen. She complimented me on being one of the "greats" whom Peter had selected, but remarked that I was the only one listed that she had never heard of. Needless to say, this brought me back to earth in a hurry. Her timing was impeccable. She had "whened" me into humility beautifully.

Tennis isn't often thought of as an art form. The science of the game is important, but when you think about it everyone has his or her own style. It's when players use what they've got that they get the most out of their game. A player may not have perfect strokes, or even one perfect stroke, but like a great artist can paint the canvas with a beautiful picture even though all the best paints, brushes, and canvases are not at his or her disposal. Another analogy would be the way a lioness stalks her prey. When she comes out of the bush too early she gives her prey the advantage. When she comes out too late she misses in another way. Tennis players must time their attack similarly so as not to overplay or underplay. Timing is everything.

This is why I feel the emphasis on "when" is crucial at all levels of tennis. The "art" or "when" is tantamount to success. The best players in the world can make most every shot. Their challenge is to make them when they are needed the most. Lesser players might need to concentrate on a certain fundamental to make a shot during a crucial point. When they do this and execute properly they have met their challenge. The timing of life's "when" challenges are also crucial to success. Whether you're a beginner or tour player, if you want to reach your full potential I think that following some of my thoughts in *WHENING* TENNIS will help you.

The game of tennis is ever changing. "When" decisions are constantly required. Whether the decisions need to be made during play or when planing play, they are part of everyone's tennis challenge.

WHENING TENNIS is a winning philosophy. When you've read this book or those sections that interest you, it is my hope that when you need to make decisions about tennis, for whatever reason, my book will help you. Enjoy.

PHASE ONE
UNDERSTANDING WHENING TENNIS

WHEN – The most important word in tennis.

One of the reasons I've felt the need to write this book is that virtually all the tennis books previously written are "how to" books. Strokes are described in great detail by many authors. I'm sure these books have been a help to thousands of players who have read them. If you read several you begin to realize that there are standards that authors agree upon for every stroke.

What then, is so important about the word "when" for tennis? First, I'm sure you'll agree that "when" is important in everything you do. Life is full of "when" decisions. All sports require myriads of "when" decisions to do almost everything. Tennis is no exception. I hope reading *WHENING* TENNIS adds a new dimension to the "how to" of playing your game.

This book will take you a step further with answers about when to do things. I will try to answer the "when" questions I've been asked over my lifetime of tennis. When should I start my child in tennis lessons? When is it better to let a lob bounce before hitting an overhead? When can a player really feel that he or she has won their match? There are an infinite number of "when" questions to be answered.

WHENING TENNIS will take you through the whole gamut of tennis, answering these and many other important questions. Hopefully, this book will help you play your best and bring you to a higher level without major changes in your strokes. Tennis is such a cerebral game. Adding the missing "when" to the "how to" will open up new possibilities for your tennis. And if you can get more mileage out of your game and make better decisions because of these answers, I will have accomplished my goal.

WIN – What can it really mean for you?

We Americans are addicted to winning and statistics. Tennis promotes this addiction by its ranking systems as well as league and tournament play at every level. It's what you want to achieve when you play, isn't it?

Or is it? I'm going to give you a new slant on winning here in *WHENING* TENNIS. I've come by this different slant honestly. As a former UCLA athlete and friend of John Wooden I'm convinced that his philosophy of being successful, which doesn't always include coming out ahead in the score, is without peer. In his book <u>Wooden</u>, which he wrote with Steve Jamison, John states that "the fundamental goal in life, as in basketball (and I will add tennis), is to make the effort to do the best you are capable of doing." He also states that "the apex of my famous pyramid is success, and true success is attained only through the satisfaction of knowing you did everything within the limits of your ability to become the very best that you are capable of being." This is what I consider to be the true meaning of winning.

No one wins every match or every tournament, but everyone who plays with their best effort is a winner. Effort is the key. Every day is going to be different, even in terms of effort. But making the effort, no matter how you feel or what the day has brought you, will allow you to do your best for that day. No matter what the score, you've won. You can proudly go on. What a great way to compete. I know this is the answer for when you really win.

I'll go into more detail about this in the section *WHENING* TENNIS – You can't do any better, in Phase Six.

John Wooden with Steve Jamison, <u>Wooden</u> (Illinois: Contemporary Books 1997)

PHASE TWO
OUR CHANGING GAME

COURT TECHNOLOGY – What has it done to our game?

Court surface really makes a difference in the strokes needed, strategy used, and even in the equipment and clothing needed to play the game. Different surfaces dictate everything. Actually, the play on clay and grass hasn't changed much over the years. The real changes have been in the modernization of surface materials for cement and asphalt courts.

You might be asking why I have brought this up? The reason is that, with extended play, the cement and asphalt courts of yesterday became very slick and played more like grass. So serve and volley was the major tactic used in those days. Also, with the exception of the French Open, all the major tournaments, Davis Cup, and Wightman Cup, were played on grass. If you didn't serve and volley you had your problems.

When silica sand was introduced into the paint surfaces for hard courts many years ago it became possible to regulate the speed of the court. As clubs, schools, and park departments became aware that courts would play slower and last longer, sand was always included in surface material specifications when courts were built or resurfaced.

The change in this court technology for cement and asphalt courts has made a major change in tennis tactics and stroke emphasis. Also, the facts that much of the world can build clay courts more economically and that grass has faded from the international scene, has put more emphasis on slower tactical play. The serve and volley tactic is tough to implement on a slower surface.

When all this is considered it's easy to understand why the game has changed so dramatically. This has affected the way professionals teach the game. It has affected the junior game, the intercollegiate game, as well as players in the professional ranks. The emphasis has shifted to the backcourt game, and the volley, I think, has lost its former importance.

This should also tell you something about your own game. When you analyze yourself and the way you are playing does your game fit the court surface you normally play? Making some changes in your thinking and possibly in the way you are developing points may enable you to defeat your archrival. You'll learn more on the changes that you might need to make in your game as I expand on this later.

LIGHTER RACKETS – An unhealthy con job, but it's correctable.

Is lighter better? It seems to be from the standpoint of the manufacturer. It sells rackets. It sells because, as a former retailer, I noticed buyers glowing over the ease of racket handling at point of purchase. They could imagine how easy the racket would be to move while playing. Since so many beginner and intermediate players hit the ball late, with a lighter racket they could just feel themselves getting ready earlier.

But what's the trade off? When buying a racket hardly anyone would realize that less mass in the racket might require more head speed in all strokes. I've always felt that a faster swing with a lighter racket is bound to be harder on elbows and shoulder joints. Just for ducks, try hitting a tennis ball with a baseball bat. You will hardly feel the impact. Then try hitting a tennis ball with a badminton racket. The ball won't go anywhere. It will feel like you're hitting a shot put ball. The extreme difference in the mass of both of these two implements demonstrates my point.

Wood rackets improved through the Kramer Autograph and Davis Imperial models. The steel Wilson T-2000, made famous by Jimmy Conners and the aluminum laminate racket Head made for Arthur Ashe offered further improvements.

For years, in many ways, I've felt that the lighter rackets offered by manufacturers has been a con job to sell more rackets. These light, extremely stiff, high energy rackets have spawned a new group of beginning players who just bump their shots. Many have lost the art of stroking the ball smoothly and struggle with blending proper spin to control the high energy. You simply couldn't "bump" shots with a wooden racket.

The down side here is that "bumping" relegates players to a plateau of mediocrity. They find themselves wanting to hit their shots but unable to control them. Then when they do discover that more spin helps their control, they overdo head speed on late contact and go out of the frying pan of "bumping" into the fire of elbow and/or shoulder pain.

On the brighter side, lighter, stiffer rackets can be customized with properly placed lead tape. Professionals at tennis specialty shops can add sufficient weight to bring your racket up to 12 or 13 ounces, which will give you the mass to stroke the ball easily. You probably can't imagine it but the great

Lighter, graphite composite frames have so much more energy than the wood and metal frames of the past, and come in various sizes and string patter ns as well.

players of yesterday had rackets weighing in the range of 14 to 16 ounces. When manufacturers have not already customized their rackets a few players on the circuit today beef them up considerably.

It's great to discover that with a heavier racket you don't have to swing as hard, that your racket will do more of the work for you. When you customize your racket in this way you will have corrected the lighter racket con job.

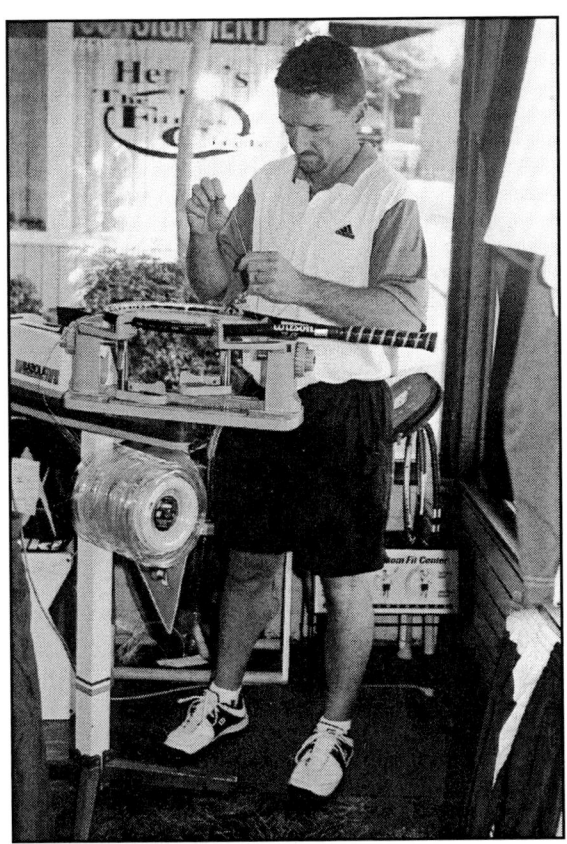

Alan Gutherie owns The Stringer, Fresno, California's premiere Tennis Shop. His skill and electronic machine make for perfect string jobs.

STRINGS CAN REALLY MAKE A DIFFERENCE – Proper selection and tension does the trick.

Tension, string design, and gauge all contribute to the "feel" of ball contact. Striking a good balance between the frame and strings is the goal. Varying the tension can help with the control and speed of your shots.

In today's market it's hard to choose because of the huge selection of strings available. The many string designs and gauges offer different playability and durability. Your tennis shop stringer can give you the options for the racket you use.

If you are one of the previously mentioned sufferers from joint problems you might consider lowering the string tension in your racket. It seems to soften the impact and make the "sweet spot" a little bigger. I've helped a number of players by restringing their racket to the 30 to 35 pound range. (Note that the normal tension range is roughly 50 to 65 pounds) It will give you a different feel with ball contact but the tradeoff has usually been rewarding with less vibration and joint pain. Of course you should still keep using your vibration dampener as well.

When you lower your string tension you'll get more of a trampoline effect when you strike the ball. This adds power that is sometimes hard to control. Real power and control naturally come from who is holding on to the racket. The strings may help a little but proper contact with the ball cannot be replaced by string tension. Power and direction are, thankfully, still in the hands of the tennis artist. You will make more of the shots you're thinking of as you improve all the aspects of proper stroking.

Some years ago I played a few tournaments on the Almaden Grand Masters Tour. The tour was put together by Al Bunis. Former world champions, Frank Sedgman, Vic Seixas, and Pancho Gonzalez, were among those who played. Beppe Merlo, an Italian champion, also played. He was a very scrappy little fellow who had his rackets strung at very low tension. He could virtually carry the ball the tension on his strings was so low. I asked him what the tension setting for his rackets was and he answered in his thick Italian accent, "Zaro." The usual "ping" was replace by "thung" when Beppe hit the ball. However, his "thung" shots were incredibly effective and everyone on the tour hated to play against him.

One last thought about strings. Remember, as much as your racket is a key element, hopefully it's the strings that actually hit the ball, not the frame. So when you buy a new racket you may have to have it strung several times to get the right kind of string and tension for your frame. Different strings have different properties, as do different tensions. When it feels good to you regardless of what someone else says, that's what you should use.

SPIN – Why is it more important now?

I've been talking about how changes in courts, rackets, and strings have changed the game of tennis. Slower courts and lighter, stiffer rackets have been the main culprits causing these changes. What then, must you do with your game to best utilize these changes to your advantage?

First you must recognize the need for more spin on the ball, especially on your forehand and backhand ground strokes.

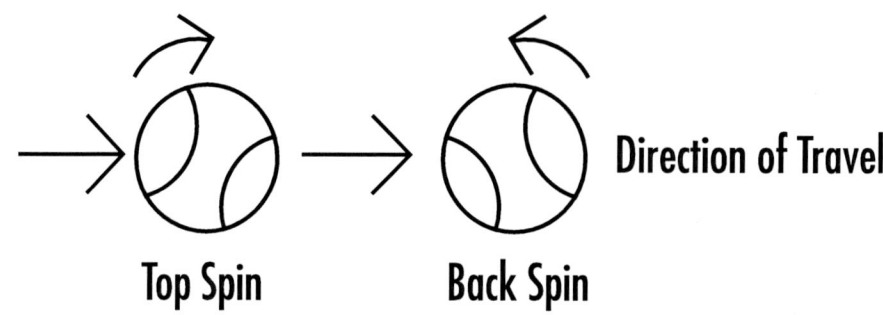

Top Spin   **Back Spin**   **Direction of Travel**

Blending the right amount of speed and spin is a must for virtually every shot.

Topspin and backspin counter the incredible energy of the modern stiff, light racket. With forehand and backhand strokes hit from the backcourt, if you give yourself enough clearance over the net, but hit a non spinning knuckle ball, it's going to fly out practically every time. A spinning ball with either topspin or backspin, creates more air resistance. As players grow in their games and begin to hit harder more spin is required for control. You must learn to "brush" or "rub" the ball to apply topspin. And equally important, you must learn to "slide" under the ball for backspin. Watch the top players. Where does their backswing start in relation to the ball contact point? Where does the followthrough finish compared to that contact point? Learning to blend the right amount of spin with the speed of each shot is part of the "art" of playing the game I talked about in my introduction.

One of the best ways to observe your stroking motion is to stand in front of a mirror at home and slowly go through each stroke. You can visualize the stroke and actually watch from start to finish. Of course, there are many other aspects to stroking, which apply spin to your shots. Changing your grip slightly will often help but we'll get to that later.

The main point I want to make here is that technology has changed how we think about tennis as well as how we play it. Spin is not a new concept. Players have applied spin to their shots since the game began. It's been primarily new racket materials and designs that have increased the need to add more spin to all shots. Spin was important with wooden rackets but it has become even more important to control the speed generated by modern composite rackets.

When these technological changes occur and changes will continue to happen, playing the game changes too. You can compare it to the changes you need to make when you play on unfamiliar courts. Adjusting to the changes is part of the challenge of playing the game.

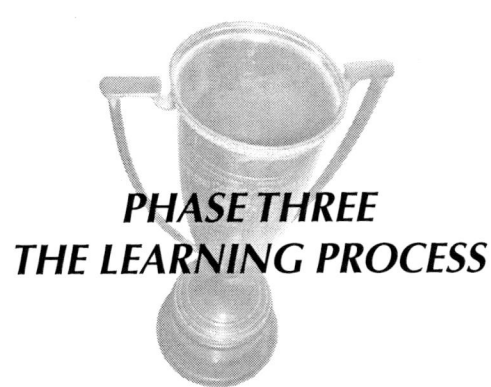

PHASE THREE
THE LEARNING PROCESS

DON'T GO IT ALONE – Teaching yourself is impossible.

You really need someone to help you with the learning process. I'm serious. If you're a beginner or if you've played for a long time but would like to improve, don't try to do it all alone. Believe me, that's why the best players in the world have coaches who follow them around the world. From week to week even professional tennis players need correction.

The bottom line is that "we can't see ourselves as others see us." So many players think they are stroking the ball perfectly. Or they think they are close enough to perfection that it doesn't matter. Close is only good for horseshoes and hand grenades. Many times being close on the execution of a certain shot is just good enough to fail, while one little change may bring success and great satisfaction.

Making these little changes is what good tennis pros do. A skilled tennis teacher knows what to look for in stroke production. Moreover, he/she can go through the steps of change which are: *Demonstration, Imitation, Correction, and Repetition.* The pro will demonstrate how the shot should be executed, have you imitate this, correct you if you aren't doing it right, and then have you repeat the stroke over and over until your "muscle memory" takes over.

The problem with doing it by yourself is that the only demonstration you can get is watching someone you think is doing it right. Then when you try to do it yourself you have no one to watch your imitation, not to mention help you correct it. The worst part of this scenario is that you'll probably repeat what you're doing wrong and just reinforce your improper muscle memory. The more you repeat a stroke incorrectly the harder it is to undo it.

Most players happily play away with what they've got. That's fine but it's really satisfying to improve, to move up to new levels. So my advice is to not try to do this without some help. Read on if you are inspired to get better, to improve and to beat that certain player or doubles team that has dominated you in past play.

A GOOD PRO IS HARD TO FIND – But worth the effort to find one.

If you're ready to take my advice as described in "Don't go it alone" let's begin to search for a good tennis teacher.

Probably your best place to start is to ask friends who have taken lessons. Some may have gone to famous tennis camps. Talking to people about the parameters of the way a pro teaches is a good start. You can certainly write off the ones who don't make the lessons fun or who ridicule your deficiencies. I like pros who are positive, who spin off your strengths to improve your weaknesses. Patience is a virtue of a good pro. Pros also need to be responsible, honest with you, and on time for lessons. As to honesty, a good pro should be forthright with you about what you do best. Everyone can't be a net rusher, but some might do better if they were. A good pro can guide a student into acquiring a proper focus. Pros who dress well demonstrate their professionalism. Pros should also keep good attendance records. This is helpful when you receive your bill and feel that you have been charged for a lesson or

Coby Roberts, the Tennis Director at the Fig Garden Swim and Racket Club in Fresno, California, has been teaching tennis for over twenty-five years. His passion for teaching the game has inspired many of his students.

lessons you did not receive. Good pros need to communicate with parents when children are taking lessons. Having a cheerful attitude and a sense of humor helps students feel more relaxed. Good pros treat everyone with the same attitude and courtesy. Last but not least a pro needs to remember everyone's name from the first lesson or clinic. These are only some of the characteristics good pros should have but they are important ones none the less.

Now let's talk about how the teaching should progress. In "Don't go it alone," I mentioned the steps of change: Demonstration, Imitation, Correction, and Repetition. Regardless of the style the pro plays, he/she should be able to demonstrate the basic fundamentals of every stroke. Pros should teach according to need, that is according to the level of play the student has reached. Tennis needs to be taught in a progressive manner. It's just like teaching math or music. Simple, basic fundamentals will carry on throughout a player's development. Louis "Satchmo" Armstrong could do whatever he wanted to with his trumpet. But he had to learn the scales first. A good pro will develop each student by starting with the basics, while also encouraging a student's natural abilities without straying from the basics.

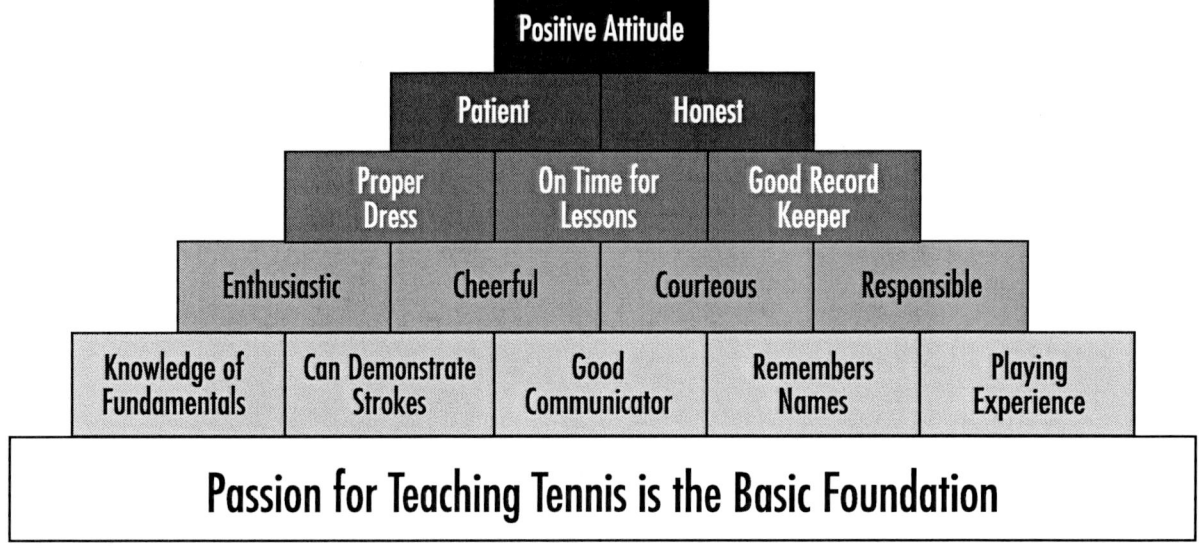

Pros that have a passion for teaching will generally exhibit many other positive traits as well.

One of the other attributes of a good pro is having played the game of tennis at a reasonably high level. Playing intercollegiate tennis, achieving state or national ranking, or playing at the professional level gives a pro insights into the game that really help even in teaching beginners. Knowing what happens out there in the upper echelons helps a pro to know how important the fundamentals are. There are many pros who haven't this valuable experience.

The USPTA and PTR are organizations in the United States that qualify persons for teaching tennis. Pros who have passed the tests offered by these two organizations will usually demonstrate the requisite professionalism. Many people apply and become qualified pros through these organizations.

Your local club or Public Park is a good place to start your search for a qualified tennis teacher. Most clubs insist that their pros have the professional qualifications required by the organizations mentioned above. And, almost every tennis club welcomes non-members to take lessons from their pros.

Also, there are famous tennis camps advertised in tennis magazines providing almost any kind of program imaginable. Mr. Charlie Hoeveler has developed his "Nike Tennis Camps" all over the United States. (Call the camp office at 1-800-Nike Camp) And, my old friend Glenn Bassett has teamed up with Billy Martin, the UCLA men's tennis coach, to provide tennis programs in the Southern California area. (Call 1-310-475-5853) There are so many US camps that it is impossible to list them all here.

My friend Peter Burwash, has developed the most comprehensive staff of tennis professionals ever assembled in Peter Burwash International. His professionals are hand picked and trained in the most meticulous manner. He has many teaching stations in the United States as well as overseas. If you are thinking about a tennis vacation or are traveling in the near future you may write to Peter's outstanding organization to inquire about these destinations. The address is: Peter Burwash International, 2203 Timberloch Pl., Suite 126, The Woodlands, TX 77380. To telephone call, 281-363-4707; or FAX 281-292-7783. Packing your tennis racket along on your next trip is easy. Your vacation may be the best opportunity you'll have to find a good tennis pro.

THE TIME/MONEY BUDGET – It's the best way to do it.

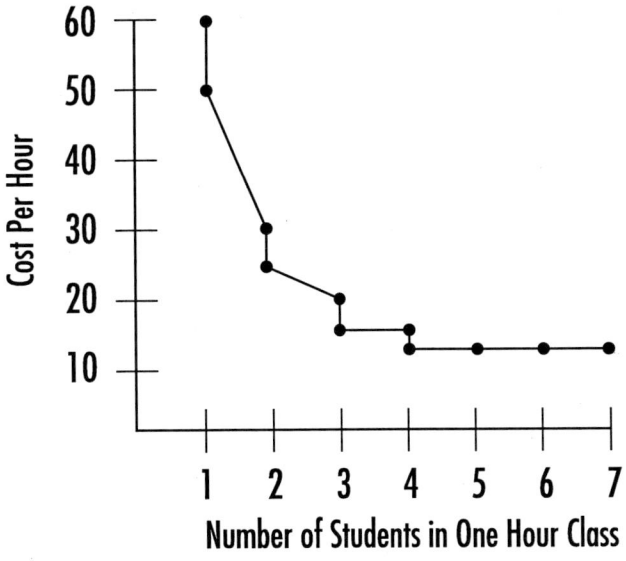

Once you've picked a pro, found out his/her fees and discussed his/her availability, you need to make a budget plan. I've had so many students who just didn't know how to proceed at this point. Some never really think about anything past taking their first lesson. I guess they think they'll play it by ear as each lesson goes along.

What you need to do is figure out how much you can afford for, say, the next two months. As an example, let's say you can afford $200 a month for this period. If private lessons are $50 each, you could take one lesson each week for two months. Group lessons and clinics cost less, so if

This chart shows the relationship of cost to the number of people in a lesson or clinic. Private lessons and clinics both have their advantages.

that's what you decide to take, then you would shuffle these figures around to suit yourself.

The next step, and it's just as important as the first, is to budget some practice time. I've always recommended a 3-to-1 ratio of practice to lessons. You must practice or you're wasting your money. Think of it as you would if you were taking music lessons. I'm sure you wouldn't dream of touching your piano only once a week at each lesson. Sometimes practice sessions are hard to prioritize into a busy schedule. I think you should wait until you have a time frame when you know you have adequate time for both lessons and practice. This budgeting process for lessons and practice applies to players of all levels.

When you have made a commitment of time and money and practice sessions you're ready to go. What's more you're giving yourself the best chance to learn. I have never turned away a request for a single lesson or casual lessons but I have often felt that this sort of an unplanned program is more harmful than beneficial. A concentrated period of lessons and practice really makes a difference. A similar situation results in dramatic improvement when skiers ski every day during a vacation. You really get a feel for the activity compared to skiing only on occasional weekends.

When you have completed your two month plan it's okay to stop for a while to practice what you've learned. If you haven't already started using a backboard or ball machine while practicing, start using them. Most clubs rent these machines, and portable, battery-operated ones are available for sale that may be used on any court. Just getting out on the court frequently with friends or by yourself will give you the repetition you need. When you reach a plateau, which everybody does as they progress, go back to your pro for another budgeted time/money session.

PRIVATE LESSONS VERSUS CLINICS – Do you really want to learn the game?

When was the last time you paid a little more to get what you wanted but were then disappointed? It rarely happens. Quality shines through every time. It does with private lessons as opposed to clinics. Don't get me wrong. I'm not opposed to clinics, they have a place. Indeed, they are cheaper-by-the-hour but their student/teacher ratio is restrictive. By this I mean, when an instructor has six or seven students instead

My daughter, Karin, and one of my granddaughters, Hallie, in a one on one private lesson.

of just one, he/she is unable to effectively teach the *Demonstration, Imitation, Correction, Repetition* steps for change. Every student has different problems for each stroke being taught. Group lessons with as few as three or four people reduce the effectiveness of the pro. That's why if you are a beginner, or if you want to correct something as an intermediate or even an advanced player, private one-on-one lessons are best.

In my "Don't Go It Alone" section I've alluded to the inefficiency of trying to teach yourself. The amazing thing is that when pros demonstrate how a certain stroke should be many people try to imitate what they see and hear but they aren't even close. The correction phase requires re-demonstration, sometimes several times, to fix the image in the student's mind. The patience of the pro is often put to the test in this process. Once the student makes the corrections and can imitate or create the stroke properly it's time for lots of repetition.

I'm a firm believer that this repetition be made as easy as possible, even for better players trying to correct something. The difficulty needs to be taken out of the situation so the student doesn't have to struggle to learn the stroke. I want my students to feel what it's like to make the stroke and shot just right so they'll know how that feels. Then when the student is ready for increased difficulty it can be added. However if muscle memory is lost by adding difficulty, you have to go back to an easier situation. Eventually as muscle memory is retained with the proper form, it can be carried into a competitive situation. In a private lesson, all of these things have a better chance of being accomplished. You're going to get the maximum bang for your buck from private lessons.

When are clinics the better vehicle? There are actually many good applications for clinics. Clinics work well, I believe, when players are reasonably

Clinics provide a social atmosphere and can be really good workouts. Cuyler Legler, teaching this group, is the head pro at Fig Garden Swim and Racquet Club in Fresno.

proficient in their basics skills. In clinics, students mostly drill strokes. Sometimes strategy is their focus. Both of these scenarios work well to fine-tune skills as long as students do not need a lot of individual help.

Another good time to use clinics is for children. There's a fun element when they're out there playing with their buddies. Also, sometimes a reluctant child will agree to start tennis if their friends are involved. There's a certain comfort for adults too, when they can go out to learn the game together. One of my favorite

Cuyler Legler and assistant pro Mary Ellen McGuire are shown here putting the kids in their clinic through some drills. Buddies often like the competitive atmosphere of clinics.

clinic times is when I get a family to take one together. A maximum of six to seven students is enough for any clinic but even more may join in so you don't have to break up the family. If people have begun tennis instruction in a clinic that's okay too. They can move up to private lessons when they reach a plateau and need individual help.

The main point I want to make here is that if you really want to learn to play tennis you must, at some point, take private lessons. Use the clinics too, in the ways I've suggested if that works for you. Most pros are very open to teach in whichever mode you want. They'll split a private lesson for two people or they seldom hesitate to take three or four people in what's called a group lesson. Clinics usually involve five or more people. In each of these different lesson plans the cost is directly related to the student/pro ratio.

COMMITMENT – It's necessary, but a lot tougher today.

Tennis looks easy. Especially when you watch the pros playing. They seem to just glide to every shot and make everything go so smoothly. I'm here to tell you that they're working their petudies off. Top tennis is a very strenuous sport. It's plain hard work out there. The pros, the national amateur level players and the intercollegiate players have worked hard to get where they are. They have paid their dues and must continue to do so to keep up, not to mention to get ahead. They had to make a commitment at sometime during their formative years to reach their level of play.

Everyone beginning tennis needs to make a commitment as well. I've described this to some extent in my section "The time/money budget," in Phase Three. The beginner's commitment isn't as deep as the pro's commitment mentioned above. But nevertheless, this is not an easy game to learn and right from the start you have to give it some special priority if you want to improve.

I just used the magic word "improve." Improving is what keeps us all in the game. No matter how good you get you always want to play better. Making the commitment to the sport of tennis will give you your best chance to improve. Whether you're just beginning to play, or trying to advance to a higher level, there needs to be a commitment to some sort of plan.

It's not easy for working adults to give tennis this priority. But it is possible to choose a time when making a commitment may be reasonable for you. The rewards are worth it for a lifetime of tennis enjoyment. However you don't have to continue the commitment when you're comfortable with the level you have reached. Everyone has fun at every level. Getting over the first hump, what I call the "ball chasing stage," requires one's first and most important commitment.

It's equally hard these days for kids to commit to tennis. There are so many activities for them in addition to their studies in school. School is absolutely the first priority. But there's soccer, music, dance, little league baseball, basketball, and football. On and on it goes. As a child I played most all of these activities myself but I was lucky in regards to tennis. My dad had a tennis shop and we lived across the street from some public courts. I couldn't help but play tennis. Most kids aren't in this situation, so the commitment is more difficult for both them and their parents.

I want to tell you a story about a young man that I taught to play tennis some years ago in Fresno. His name is Larry Hall. As a youngster he was a fabulous athlete. So, naturally, he was a pleasure to teach. Also, he was really committed to learning the game.

Fresno is a foggy place in winter because it's located in the Central Valley of California between the Sierra Nevada on the east and the Coast Range on the west. Even in this cold, damp weather, Larry, at ten or eleven years old, would ride his bike out to the public courts where I taught. He was always there before I was, just sitting there in the fog, shivering, waiting for me to arrive.

He became a fine player for his college tennis team at Brigham Young University and he was an All-American in 1970. Then he became the head professional at a prestigious club in Jackson, Mississippi. After that he became the men's tennis coach at his alma mater where he still works as a professor. His commitment to tennis not only helped him become a fine player, it added to his life in many ways. You too could be pleasantly surprised as well with whatever level of commitment you may make to tennis.

For some reason it seems that parents sign their kids up for tennis when they haven't been able to make the team for soccer, baseball, or another sports team. Now I don't mean to discourage parents from doing this but I want them to realize that tennis is probably one of the hardest sports, if not the hardest, to learn. It's not like playing shuffleboard or marbles, believe me. Even good athletes sometimes struggle to learn tennis. And they need commitment as much as any other athlete.

My point in this section is to stress the importance of commitment if you want to learn to play tennis. As I mentioned above, when you make a commitment, you've given yourself the best chance to improve in this wonderful lifetime game.

PARENTS ARE NECESSARY FOR KIDS – In more ways than one.

In Phase Three, which I titled "The Learning Process," I have included this "Parents Are Necessary" section for a very important reason. Kids have a very difficult time learning tennis without help from an adult. It doesn't have to be a parent or a guardian. But somebody needs to help with the money, transportation, and mostly, the practice.

I have already mentioned my 3-to-1 practice to lesson ratio. For this ratio to happen someone

Chase Huebner's Aunt Karin is helping him hit his forehand. With kids this young you have to be close enough to toss the ball softly.

has to get out there and do these practice sessions with the kids. A big brother or sister can often fill the bill. Children who are just learning, even the little 4-year-olds, need someone to bounce the balls to them. That's how it starts. Later you may be rallying together. And still later, if things go right, you'll be playing together.

Without realizing it at first, you may be creating a future playing partner. I can tell you first hand this reward is most satisfying. Again, I was lucky in this regard because as my kids were growing up I was a tennis pro. But I had to work with all three of them just as I'm suggesting for you to do. It's amazing but it really doesn't take long to get so you can enjoy some rallies with them. I now have the great pleasure of playing, with some success, in national doubles tournaments with each of my three children.

I'm not going to dwell on this but I've seen how quickly kids mature when they have an adult to help them. The pro can't do it all. Sometimes he/she can help by introducing other kids to practice with yours. This helps. However, again I can tell you from my own experience, the rewards far outweigh the effort it takes to help your kids learn the game.

Beanie Irola practicing with her grandson, Vincent, and her granddaughter, Leslie at the Fig Garden Swim and Racquet Club in Fresno, California.

SAS – The only way to fly.

You're probably thinking that I'm pushing Scandinavian Airlines here, but even though I'm sure they are a wonderful airline this is not a commercial. SAS is included in "The Learning Process" because I believe the letters stand for how the learning process should proceed. When tennis players are learning they need some guidelines. SAS is a guideline for learning every stroke including the serve.

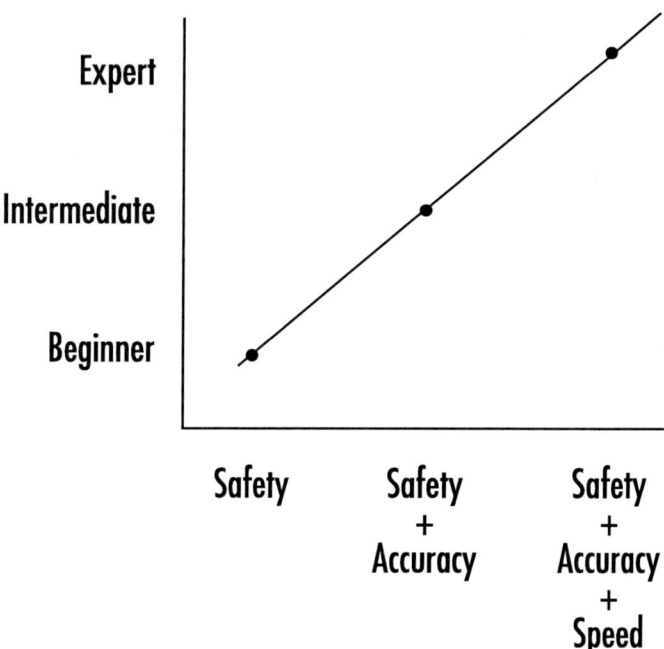

Everyone wants to play like a pro. Some players hit shots with speed and placement even the pros wouldn't try. My advice is to follow SAS in learning and perfecting all your strokes. Here's how SAS works.

The first letter "S" stands for *safety*. As you are learning to perfect each stroke you must make an effort to play your shots safely over the net within the boundary of the court. Often people get ahead of themselves. First, you must be able to hit a forehand or backhand over the net into the center of the opposite court. You must also be able to serve over the net into the center of the opposite service court. And so on with all the strokes.

Now when you when you are able to safely play a given shot as described above, you may add the "A" word, *accuracy*, to your shots. Go back to your forehand now and hit some crosscourt

You'll progress best if you keep SAS in mind. Keeping the ball in play is the bottom line for percentage tennis.

shots, without sacrificing safety. When you can safely hit your serve and other shots add the accuracy factor to them.

Finally, when you can hit consistently with both safety and accuracy you're ready to add the final "S" which, by now you've probably guessed, is *speed*. Only a few students need to be told to hit harder. When players feel right about the safety and accuracy of their shots they just naturally add more power to them.

The reason I developed this SAS formula is that so many players of all levels, not just beginners, try to hit too hard. I think men are more guilty of this than women. Uncontrolled shots flying all over the court produce very few points. Also, it's not much fun rallying with someone who hits this way either. Haven't you watched people serve as hard as they can on their first serve? Then they just wimp the second one. And the rallies only last for one or two shots at most. Percentage tennis can't be played this way.

I had one student who hit every shot, with horrible form I must add, as hard as he could. I tried to get him to slow down to get some shots into the court but he kept blasting every ball. Finally, I asked him why he wanted to hit so hard. He said his high school coach told him to do it. I then asked if his coach had a reason for telling him this. His answer was, " The coach told me that was the way the pros did it so I should do it too." I was amazed that his coach would tell him this. This is like a music teacher telling a new student to blow as hard as possible on a trumpet and eventually good sounds will come out.

The bottom line is that when you can safely and accurately hit a certain shot you will naturally add speed. Just make sure the first "S" for your shots is safety, not speed.

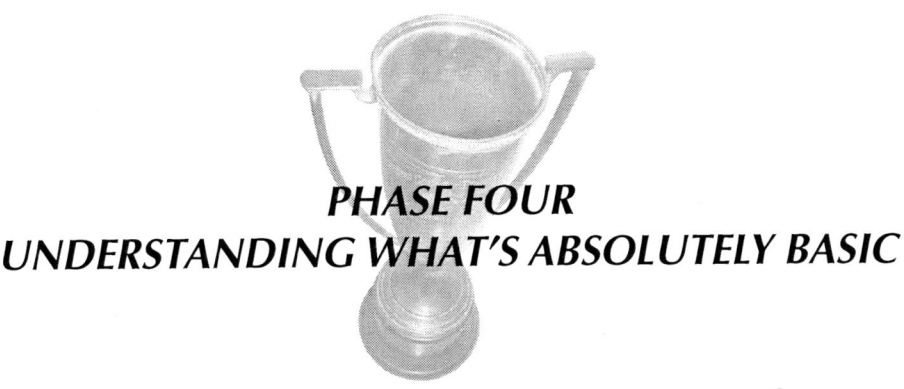

PHASE FOUR
UNDERSTANDING WHAT'S ABSOLUTELY BASIC

PERCENTAGE TENNIS – Why is it so important?

Errors are a bigger part of tennis than winning placements. In statistics kept for most matches players make more errors than they make winners. If this is true at top levels of the game what would the ratio of errors to winning placements be for your game? You may not want to know but even if you don't want to actually compute the ratio it's enough to know that it is a crucial part of everyone's game. Improving just a fraction in this ratio can mean dramatic advancement at most every level of play.

There are two kinds of errors that are mostly talked about. One, of course, is when your opponent forces you to miss your return shot. The other is when you miss a shot that you should have made. This last error is called "unforced." But there is another description of errors that I feel is very important, especially for players new to the game. I want to talk here about "good" errors and "bad" errors in regards to percentage tennis.

Basically, there are two ways to make an error with a tennis shot. You can hit the ball out of court or into the net. In either case you lose the point. But one of the errors is better than the other, percentage wise. You might want to think about this for a moment. Ok, your moment is up – which is it?

That's right – you got it. Hitting the ball out of court is the better error. Why? It's because you got the ball over the net. A ball going into the net has no possibility to ever be a successful shot. Once a ball goes into the net play is all over isn't it? But if you clear the net your ball has a chance. A strong wind might even blow it back in if it's headed out. When you give yourself a clearance of four to five feet over the net, ("margin for error" is what I like to call it), your shot has passed the first test. It may not go in but it had a chance. You have played the percentages correctly. Clearing the net is, of course, only the first challenge. Keeping the shot within the playing boundaries is the second, important challenge.

You need to understand this simple "bad and good error" business because it's basic to understanding the fundamentals of forehands, backhands, and serves. It's going to make stroke production logical and understandable. We're going to discuss this in detail later.

WATCH THE BALL – It's still as important as it ever was.

"Watch the ball" is a phrase that is as old as the game. It has, however, been maligned of late by a number of pros who say it doesn't really apply because seeing the ball at contact is impossible. I read a magazine article recently in which a well known pro described "watching the ball" as a tennis myth. He said the ball was traveling too fast to be seen on contact. I'll give him that but I believe watching the ball to contact with the strings is still absolutely basic. I call it "keeping your head on the ball" and this applies to all tennis shots including the serve.

Players who do not follow the ball-to-racket contact have difficulty adjusting to different court speeds, spins of the ball, or to bad bounces on clay or grass courts. Almost without exception, the great players of the game "watch the ball" to contact with the racket. It's a requirement for every stroke: from serving, where it helps you keep your head up, to volleys and ground strokes, where following the ball maximizes "sweet spot" contact. When you're "head is on the ball," not looking to where you're directing your shot, it helps greatly to disguise your intentions. I don't think players realize that looking up before contact on ground strokes telegraphs to the opponent where the shot is headed.

Another plus I've discovered when I "watch the ball" to the racket is that it seems to slow everything down. I actually feel I have more time, especially on service returns. Also when players "watch the ball" coming off their opponent's racket and respond quickly, there is more time to get ready for the next shot. I call it "watching the ball from racket to racket."

I have a student, Hank Palmer, who is a good 4.5 NTRP (National Tennis Rating Program) player. Though he started tennis late in life, Hank is a good athlete who has made a commitment to improve his game.

In one of our lessons I suggested this "watch the ball" exercise to keep his "head on the ball." Hank had been doing it with his serve which greatly helped him to be more consistent with that shot. He told me that, when he kept his head up while serving, he got a visual picture of the sky. If he didn't get this picture Hank knew he had probably pulled his head down.

On forehands and backhands, when Hank watched the ball to contact, he had a picture of the ball "streaking to the racket and streaking out from it." This visualization again told Hank that he had, indeed, "kept his head on the ball." Hank said he had never experienced this visualization before on his groundstrokes but that it made a tremendous difference in his feel for the ball and its contact with the racket.

I asked Hank, as I often do other students, if doing so made groundstrokes feel different from his previous groundstrokes. His answer was that it did feel really different. I explained that when you change something like this it will feel differently. Thus proving that it wasn't something he was doing before.

I advised Hank to "watch the ball" to the racket on all strokes while warming up before every match. When I do this it has always started

Tony Trabert, an old friend, won five singles World Championship Grand Slams by keeping his eye on the ball to contact.

me off correctly and carried into the match. I advise you to practice this and do the same.

So my advice may be contrary to some pros' ideas about "watching the ball" but you will greatly benefit in many ways, I believe, by following this important rule of tennis. It's absolutely basic.

PLAYING THE BALL – Not letting the ball play you.

I remember the first time I played a game of squash. I felt like a cat chasing it's tail as I tried to judge the ball coming off the walls. I was definitely not in control. The ball was playing me, and it was a helpless feeling.

A lot of tennis players suffer from the same feeling of helplessness. They want to have the ball in the right spot to hit it but they really don't know where that spot should be. I think I can help you with this.

Imagine a ball coming across the net to you. When it bounces it makes an arc before bouncing again. In a backcourt rally most balls will bounce as high as your knees or waist. Sometimes it's lower or higher but there's always this nice, semicircle arc when it bounces.

For your forehand or backhand you need to move to a spot where you can hit the ball just as it comes over the top of its bounce. It's beginning to descend at this point. If your

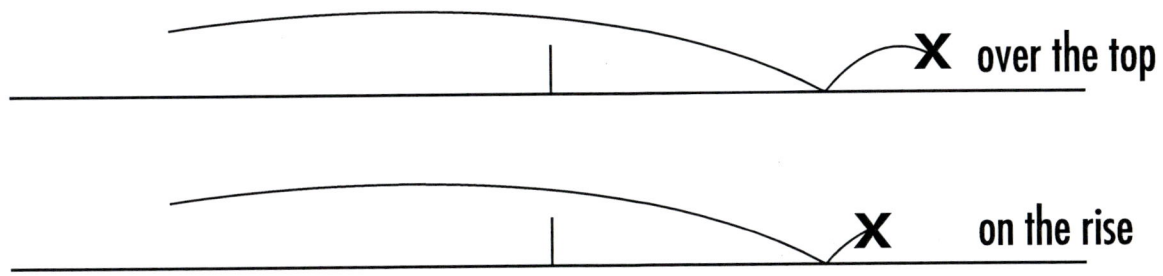

Knowing where you want the ball to be when you make contact is the first step. Judging it's flight, and then getting in position to meet the ball just over the top of the bounce are the next steps for an easier groundstroke. Hitting "on the rise" is more difficult.

stroke has started forward from below the ball as it should, you'll be on a perfect collision course with the ball as you meet it on the way up in your follow through. Notice how this blends in with aiming 4 to 5 feet over the net to get the "margin for error" I spoke of in the "Percentage Tennis" section. Stroking from "low to high" as most pros describe it, makes good contact possible on both forehands and backhands, especially when the ball is contacted just over the top of the bounce.

Another tip is to make ball contact early, out in front if possible. "Out in front" means to make contact before the ball passes by your forward leg. This presumes that you have made your turn to get into position to hit the ball. Even if you hit with what's called an "open stance" you should still not let the ball get behind you.

The two key things here are judgement of ball speed and its direction and "getting the lead out" to move to the ball. Now you know where you want the ball to be to hit it, you just have to get there.

The term I use for getting to this spot is "trapping the ball." It puts you in a position so that you'll be on good balance and be able to adjust at the last second, if necessary, so as not to let the ball get behind you. For either backhands or forehands you must make the extra effort to get your back foot placed pretty much in line with the ball coming to you. When you do this you have the flexibility to either step into the shot (closed stance) or step away from the shot (open stance). This is especially helpful for dealing with bad bounces or when it's windy. Of course, you can't be in this position all the time. It requires an earlier extra step to get to the ball, which may be a luxury you won't always have. However, when you can "trap the ball" you'll be able to push off your back leg as you meet the ball out in front and you'll really "get some stick" into your forehand or backhand drive.

I've often used the word "vector" to describe the direction from the center of your body (your belly button) to the ball contact point. As you grow in the game you'll instinctively know just how far away, at what part of the bounce and how far in front you want the ball on all shots. As you achieve a sense of this "vector" it becomes more a part of your shot production and you will become much more consistent. You'll be playing the ball, not letting the ball play you.

Three improper "vectors" come to mind. One is when a player runs too close to where the ball will likely bounce. In this case, the ball is what we call "on the rise" and expert timing is required to hit it properly. It is often "miss hit." Players who do this often hit the ball too far behind themselves as well. The second instance is when players in a net position volley the ball too far back. Players consistently "miss hit" this shot. The third example is when the ball has been tossed poorly during serving. Many players move their feet to go after these bad tosses, which causes a lot of serving errors.

In each of these examples the "vector" from player to ball wasn't right. Maybe the stroke was okay but not playing the ball properly created an error. You must first judge where you need to be and then time your move so you can reach out when a perfect "vector" to the ball presents itself.

It goes without saying that you can't play the ball where you want it every time. But if you know where you want it to be, you have solved part of the problem. The other part of the problem is the challenge to get to the right spot to have that little orb where you want it. Again, if you do this you will be playing the ball, not letting the ball play you. I'll talk about why the ball should be played "out front" on almost every stroke in the next section.

THE BALL CONTACT POINT – Out in front on most shots is best.

When golfers hit their shots they stand sideways. Baseball players do the same. Quarterbacks drop back to pass in a sideways stance. Why do all these sports require this sideways stance? The simple answer is to get body weight transfer into whatever they're doing. When you don't use this valuable lever you're not going to get the most out of your golf shot, your baseball swing or throw, or your football pass. It's the same in tennis. Even a little weight transfer helps with virtually every tennis shot.

Now the stance for tennis can be a little different. Balance is the operative word. You may place your feet in a variety of positions for tennis shots as long as you're on good balance.

The secret to transfer body weight into your forehand, backhand, serve, volley, or overhead is to meet the ball out in front. The real test for this is to notice where your weight is when you finish your shot. Has it transferred from your back foot to your front foot? When it has you must have hit the ball fairly far forward or the weight wouldn't have been transferred. Try tossing a ball up behind you on serve. Then hit it. Did your weight transfer to your front foot. I don't think so. If you do this on forehands, backhands, and

Correct forehand contact out in front versus incorrect late contact.

Correct backhand contact out in front versus incorrect late contact.

Correct service contact out in front versus incorrect contact too far back.

Correct volley contact out in front versus incorrect late contact.

volleys, weight transfer will not happen either.

I was talking to my old high school pal Steve Blumberg about this and he pointed out how important the timing of weight transfer is. He feels that the transfer has to be part of forward stroke motion. I couldn't agree with him more. I think hitting the ball out in front really helps tell you when to make your weight move forward. However, placing weight on your front foot too early misuses this weight transfer lever and just leaves you swinging with your arm.

My daughter, Karin, played her intercollegiate tennis at UCLA. She captained the team to the NCAA championship in 1981. Then, she spent several years on the WTA tour. So, she has earned her stripes to be a tennis coach. She has a little trick for learners wherein she instructs them to "hit and point" for their forehands and backhands. This helps beginning players transfer their weight to their front foot while pointing their back foot as they finish the shot. It's something like your form when you finish bowling a ball down the alley. You should try this if you're having trouble with weight transfer. You'll find out that you can't have any weight on your back foot when you "hit and point."

The main point that I want you to pick up here is that, in tennis, you don't do everything with your arm. Indeed, the shoulder, elbow, and wrist are all levers that need to be used, but you can't get the most out of them without weight transfer. This is possible only when you meet the ball out in front. The only exception to this is the backhand slice or chip shot, which I'll cover later.

Karin's weight has shifted forward which has left her right toe pointing down during "hit and point" practice.

When you meet the ball "out in front" on your backhand, your back foot "points" just as it will on your forehand.

THE READY POSITION – When not having one really hurts.

When you are waiting for your opponent's serve or you're in a rally you don't have the luxury of standing sideways, you must be ready to move either way. A good ready position for tennis requires you to face forward. But that's not all.

You must hold your racket up with both hands in front of you. Two-handed players hold the racket with both hands on the grip. One-handers should have their playing hand on the grip and the other hand at the throat of the racket. The non-dominant hand is very important. First, the non-dominant hand helps hold the racket head up higher than the

A good "backcourt" ready position will allow you to move with equal quickness to your forehand or backhand.

Keeping your racket head up with your opposite hand will get you started correctly for grip change and stroke preparation.

Most two fisted players hold both hands on the racket handle. As two hand players improve some will play a ready position more like a one hander, and then slide their non-dominant hand down to set their grip.

grip or handle of the racket. Second, the non-dominant hand helps you change your grip for different shots. For one-handers it's a must to change from a forehand grip, which is what you hold in the ready position, to a backhand grip. Most two handers change their dominant-hand grip slightly when they hit their two-hand backhands.

It's amazing to me how many players have poor ready positions. I don't think they realize that a poor ready position contributes to late contact with the ball. Late contact can, unfortunately, translate into painful elbow and shoulder problems. This is when not having a good ready position really hurts.

Getting quickly back to a good ready position between every shot, volleys included, is absolutely basic. Just doing it will often correct the problem of late hitting of both forehands and backhands.

If you take my advice here and make the effort to start each point or rally with a good ready position and then come back to it after each shot as the rally proceeds, you'll be doing yourself a favor. If you do this and it feels sort of strange, it's a sign you probably haven't been holding a good ready position between all shots. Keep thinking about it and doing it until "muscle memory" takes over. Then it will be automatic. You'll be giving yourself the best chance to hit your shots out in front as described in "Playing The Ball" and in "The Ball Contact Point." Transferring your weight takes a lot of strain off of your elbow, believe me.

I like to teach a little higher ready position when you're at the net volleying. You'll be surprised at how much easier it is to move your racket to the ball when you do this. In this position your racket handle should be about as high as the net. Also, your racket head should be held almost vertically over your playing hand on the grip. You need to teach yourself to place your non-playing hand at the throat of the racket to hold up the head of the racket. When you hold your ready position too low during volleys you'll have a harder time meeting the ball out in front.

SOUND FUNDAMENTALS – Learn them to stay healthy – and play better.

If you're with me so far you've already got a handle on some of the most important tennis fundamentals. You're probably curious about the "stay healthy" part of this heading. Normally, most players would agree that good fundamentals will help you play better but why would they keep you healthier?

From time to time there are going to be injuries playing any sport. They seem to go with the territory. Ankles get sprained, knees get twisted, and blisters pop up. These cannot be avoided by having a more perfect tennis stroke. You play the game, you take your chances with these, okay?

What I'm talking about are mainly the pesky strains that develop in elbows and shoulders. Sometimes people whack themselves with forehand follow-throughs and hit themselves on the lower leg while serving. All these injuries are definitely bad for your health. They can be avoided when you learn better fundamentals. The worst injury can happen when players do not move back properly for an overhead. When they haven't been taught to turn sideways in order to back up, a very hard, possibly dangerous fall may result. Let's take these concerns one at a time to see what we can do to avoid them:

Tennis elbow and shoulder are simply strained, inflamed tendons. How did they get strained and inflamed? I think that hitting the ball late is the main culprit. When you hit the ball late, as I said in both the "Ball Contact Point" and "Ready Position" sections, you can't get your weight to help you. When you try to make up for this with a faster swing or more muscle you're going to strain something. Get ready earlier. Hit the ball out in front, smoothly.

Have you whacked yourself lately? Please, if you're doing this on forehands or backhands, you're not hitting through the ball contact point properly. You're also probably expending too much energy after ball contact. That's why the racket has come back to "nail" you. Think about this. Doesn't the ball leave the racket immediately upon contact? Well, if it does, what good does it do to be so violent in the follow-through? The ball is already gone. What you need to do is back up your timing so that your main force is behind the contact point. Then when you stay in the hitting zone longer, your follow-through will just float to a finish. Try it, you'll like it. Best of all you won't be whacking yourself any more.

If you've hit yourself in the shins while serving you could use a serving lesson. I'm always amazed at how many players think that a serve is a shot where you toss the ball up and then hit it down into the service court. If this is what you're trying to do you've got more than one problem.

There are a number of serving fundamentals you may need to bone up on. The first one is that serves need topspin to allow you to clear the net comfortably (see "clearance over the net" and "margin for error" in the "Percentage Tennis" section of Phase Four) and at the same time come down into the service court. Obviously, to impart forward spin (topspin), you have to hit up at the ball. If you do this and pronate your wrist after contact with the ball you won't hit your leg any more. Moreover, you won't break as many rackets that have slipped out of your grip on the downswing. This is only a cursory-coverage of serving. There are more basics that will enlighten you if you take some serving lessons.

Good preparation for your overhead requires getting sideways with your racket up over your shoulder and pointing your left hand at the ball.

If you don't turn sideways you're asking for trouble. If you don't point toward the ball with your non-playing hand other problems can occur.

Last but certainly not least, in this "stay healthy with good fundamentals sermon" is proper preparation when going back for a lob. It's easy. When you see the lob go up (presumably you're in a good ready position facing the net), you must take a step back as you raise your racket over your shoulder. If you are right-handed you should step back with your right foot and raise your racket over your shoulder with your right hand at the same time. Now you're in position to "slide back," I call it, as you would in basketball. Or, imagine yourself as a quarterback in football dropping back to pass. I teach "step back, racket up, slide back." You should drill this until it becomes automatic for you. I shudder every time I watch players who don't do this properly. It's also good to point your left hand at the ball when you do this. It will help you keep your eye on the ball and stay on balance.

Now don't you feel better already? Just kidding. I am serious, though, about how fundamentals help in this area. You would have to get pretty far afield of the basics to fall into one of these situations mentioned above. But I wouldn't have brought them up if I hadn't seen a number of these unhealthy happenings. Good fundamentals really do keep you healthier and enable you to play better.

FOOTWORK – Moving your feet for good balance.

When beginners watch tennis experts they are often impressed with their beautiful strokes and service motions. Great footwork is rarely praised. However, tennis is a game played mainly with the lower body. Moving your feet is the name of the game. I'll be talking about foot movement in several sections of this book but there are some specific things about moving your feet that need to be emphasized.

When people begin to learn tennis groundstrokes and volleys their coaches must make it easy for them by tossing or hitting balls in perfect positions to hit. When students become comfortable with these strokes, that is when correct strokes are learned, then a more difficult challenge is necessary. The coach should start to toss or hit balls so the student has to move to hit the shots. I've always explained to students that if they move to the ball early, with good timing and on balance, it's no harder to hit these shots than when the ball is coming right to them. This is the challenge they'll have as long as they play the game.

Learning to start early with either sliding steps or outright running and then shortening steps as the proper position is reached, is the goal of good movement for groundstrokes.

For volleys students must learn what's called a "split step." This is actually a slight hop with both feet at the same time so quick movement can be made in either direction. Good players do this "split step" while returning serve and between groundstroke rallies as well. You should also use this "split step" when you follow your serve into the forecourt in both singles and doubles. Seeing this demonstrated is easier to visualize than reading about it. If your pro hasn't shown you the "split step" you should ask him/her to demonstrate it.

Of course, foot movement is important throughout a match. But there are two times during a match when, I think, extra concentration on moving your feet is important. The first time is while you're warming up. Getting yourself into the match with hard working feet (after a pre-match warm-up) will set the tone for the match and get you started on the first point.

The second time you'll need to concentrate on moving your feet more is when you are falling off your game and your shots aren't doing their normal damage. This often happens when your opponent starts to move ahead in the score and/or you have begun to play tentatively. Making an extra effort to move your feet will help you get your playing engine started again.

Different court surfaces will sometimes require slightly different foot movements. Some clay courts require a sliding technique for effective foot movement. Moist grass courts can sometimes be slippery so smaller steps can help prevent falls. Hard courts, like cement and asphalt, have the best traction for longer steps but you have to be careful to buy shoes that have the proper edge design. Rolling your ankle because the shoe you selected had "catchy" edges or wasn't supportive enough is a bummer.

Quick feet are a real asset to any tennis player. If you would like to improve your own footwork you should start a routine of jumping rope. Regular use of this aerobic device can correct lazy foot problems.

Improving your footwork will definitely help you be on balance for better shot-execution. And, when you're in position earlier, you'll have more options for shot selection. I'll describe more of this in the "Anticipation and Foot Speed" section of championship requirements in Phase Seven.

GRIPS – What do they do?

When you hit your different strokes your hand/hands are the link between your mind and the racket face's contact with the ball. Your grip and stroke are going to translate into a blend of power and spin that is applied to the ball. I've already talked about why spin has become so important in today's game. And in this section, I'm going to talk about basic grips used for each stroke. Before we go further though, I want to explain what the grips do for the different strokes and what happens when grips are modified to fit the mechanics of your stroke.

• VOLLEY – When you play a position close to the net you need a grip that can be used for both forehand and backhand volleys. The grip needs to make it easy to volley up on low shots as well as to impart a slight backspin on the ball. This continental grip will be explained in Phase Five. Modifying this grip for higher forehand volleys and stroke volleys allows players to put topspin on volleys when needed.

• FOREHAND – For this shot many grips are used. Basically, it comes down to what feels comfortable for each player. When the palm of your hand is placed on the side of the grip more power can be applied. When the palm of the hand is shifted under the handle more spin is possible. Your hand's position on the handle makes it either easier to push the racket head forward or pull it up. The mechanics of the stroke are therefore vitally affected by one's grip. I think each person's strength and bone structure has much to do with what feels comfortable.

• BACKHAND – Delivering a backhand drive requires the same racket contact as a forehand drive. However, it just can't be done with the same grip. For right handers the grip must be moved to the left and conversely for lefthanders it must be moved right. The backhand grip needs to make it comfortable to push the racket head forward and pull it up as noted above for the forehand. People who use a two-handed grip make this combination easier to achieve. For both one-handers and two- handers the dominant hand needs to be in position to hit an under spin slice or a chip shot if necessary.

• SERVE – The service grip is normally the same as the volley grip. Sometimes it is modified slightly to achieve different results but it can't be changed too much or service variety is compromised. The proper service hitting motion is upward from behind the person's back to a ball tossed to a comfortable height. Just like the forehand and backhand this striking motion is needed to impart topspin to the service shot. When less spin and more power is needed the grip shouldn't be changed. It's the pronation (inward rolling) of the wrist that one needs to learn to impart more power.

Most professionals use accepted standards when they teach their students grips for different tennis shots. As players grow in their games they modify these starting grips to fit their needs. The whole process is a work in progress to blend the right amount of power and spin to the shot needed at any particular moment during play. During points players need to adjust this blend as shot selection requires. When players are able to do this at will they will have reached a high plateau and of ability to play tennis. When players can make grip changes without even thinking about them the link between thinking and executing shots becomes automatic. One's grip literally makes your racket head an extension of your thought process, enabling you to instinctively connect with the ball.

PHASE FIVE
EVERYTHING SHOULD MAKE PERFECT SENSE

UNDERSTANDING THE STROKES – They're very logical.

As we start this section, I'd like for you to keep in mind that this is a "when" not a "how to" book on tennis. There are many "how to" books available. One of the best is Tennis for Life written by my friend Peter Burwash. It has sold over one million copies and is readily available at most bookstores. I'm going to try to stick with "when" for most of my explanations. However, I'll have to put some "how to" into the mix when I explain the logic of tennis strokes.

Most of what follows presumes you have played at least a little tennis and that everything is not perfect with all your strokes. Or maybe you would like to improve certain things to gain better results. If you're just starting perhaps the logic of these explanations will help you understand how to develop your own strokes.

When you approach your game with a basic logic for each stroke the mechanics will make sense. Your preparation, your grips, the racket's attitude at contact, your timing, and

In the volley ready position you should be stationed over the center service line with your racket held up as shown.

Station yourself about two-thirds of the service court back from the net with a nice angle between your forearm and the racket. Up on your toes, ready for the volley!

Peter Burwash and John Tullius, Tennis for Life (New York: Times Books 1981)

your follow through are largely dictated by what was talked about in Phase Four that explored what's absolutely basic.

In that part of this book I noted how important "margin for error" and "hitting the ball out in front" are. I also talked about how the ball "contact point" should be just over the top of the bounce for forehand and backhand drives. Making your toss on serve and meeting your volley "out front" were also noted as important. Let's take a look at the strokes now with a view to follow these basics to develop the proper fundamentals for each stroke.

• VOLLEY - You might be a little surprised that I'm starting with this shot but it's really the easiest one. Little folks can realize their first success standing close to the net to hit their first tennis shots. It's a logical start because you don't even need a backswing to hit a volley. Think of it this way, you are much closer to your opponent when you are positioned at the net, so you don't have time to take a big backswing. Secondly, you don't need a backswing when you're this close to the net. All you need to do is use the speed of the oncoming ball to "block" it back over the net. It's much like catching a ball.

When playing volleys you should station yourself about 2/3 of the distance from the net to the service line. Don't get too close to the net when you're stationing yourself to volley so you can protect the lob. You should, of course, be straddling the center service line and facing forward. You should also be holding your ready position higher than you would in the backcourt. Your non-playing hand should hold the racket head almost vertically over your grip.

If you're holding the racket with what's called a continental grip, i.e., half way between your forehand and backhand grips, all you have to do is what I call "open the face of the racket." That's pretty easy to do on your forehand volley. You'll do this easily on the backhand volley too, if you use both hands. It's also important on the backhand volley to turn your side. You can't be facing the net and make a

Use a continental grip and keep a good angle between your forearm and your racket when you prepare to volley.

Keep the angle for the forehand volley. Don't flop the racket head forward.

Hold the angle through the finish of the backhand volley also. When you learn the chip backhand from the backcourt, this shot will be much easier.

good backhand volley. It's also important on the backhand side to release the non-playing hand when you block the volley. Two-handers struggle with this the most.

You should also hold your racket head a little higher than the expected point of ball contact. Volleys often have a slight downward motion as you block forward. This action imparts an under spin to the ball which helps you control the shot. And, as you get better, you can use the underspin to make more effective drop volleys.

For beginners the

hardest part of learning to make a backhand volley is keeping the racket head above the handle. The racket should form about a 45-degree angle with your forearm, about the same as it is in the ready position. You've got to keep this position throughout the blocked volley. Your must not allow your racket head to flop forward. Lots of people do this. When you feel the ball hit your strings you need to stop everything. Don't flop your racket at the ball.

One of the images I often suggest to volleyers is to imagine yourself in a ready position with a glass wall between your hands and your body. Your hands must stay in front of this wall as you open the face of the racket for either a forehand or backhand volley. Now with your hands out in front of the "wall," you'll easily meet the ball "out in front." Taking your racket behind the "wall" will cause you to meet the ball too late. You'll "miss hit" frequently because you can't possibly turn your head fast enough to follow the ball when it's too far behind you. The key here is that you can watch the ball to contact when you meet it "out in front." Also, you'll be able to see the court with your peripheral vision when you meet the ball "out in front."

A ready position with the "glass wall" drawn in.

The "glass wall" has moved forward and the volley is contacted nicely "out in front".

Again, the "wall" has moved forward, and the backhand volley contact was kept in front of the "wall".

Another thing I want to stress when volleying is foot movement. You must be bouncing; you must be on your toes. With small children we do "happy feet." This is actually doing what is called a constant "split step." Doing this enables you to react quickly to move forward when you volley. "Closing the net" or "cutting the corner" is what it is called. You want to step forward with the opposite foot. Right-handers step forward with their left foot for forehand volleys, their right foot for backhand volleys. When you are playing at the net the ball gets to you much more quickly. You need to react in a split second.

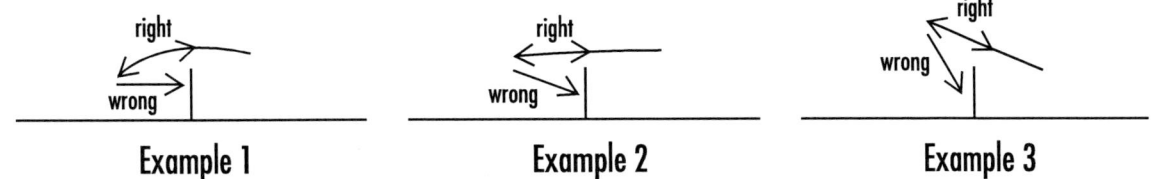

Try to hit your volleys back on about the same plane as the ball comes over the net. Changing the angle too much can cause volley errors.

My final admonition to you for better volleying is to volley back in the same plane as the ball comes over the net to you. Think about it. If the ball comes over a certain way it can be volleyed back on that same plane. Too many times I have watched volleyers try to angle the shot down too much or take a dropping ball and volley it back too straight. Often, you can change the angle slightly but be careful not to change the angle too much.

• FOREHAND – Now you will need some back swing. You're farther away from the net and from your opponent. You need to propel the ball with more zip so a back swing helps you to do this.

How you do this and how far you take your racket back is important. From a forward-facing ready position, a straight back movement of the racket as you turn you body is good for beginners. However, as players get a little better, I like them to "round out" their back swing slightly before bringing it forward. I want players to do this so that the swing is made with one motion. If you think about it, a straight-back racket motion needs to stop at the end of it's swing and then start forward again. Thus, there are two motions. You can do this in one motion if you round it out a little. I tell my students to think of swinging around a small alarm clock at their side. It's not Big Ben, so a large circle back swing isn't necessary or helpful. Actually all you have to do is to turn, keeping your ready position, and then just extend the racket head until it is pointing back at the fence behind you. The logo on the butt of your racket will now be pointing at the ball so your wrist will be slightly bent back. Your elbow should be fairly close to your body. As you round out under six o'clock at the bottom of the back swing you'll be coming up to meet the ball as it begins to descend over the top of its bounce. Voila! You're on a perfect collision course with the ball and lifting your stroke to give yourself the "margin for error" over the net that I've been talking about. You should finish your follow-through somewhat higher than the flight of the ball. This "low to high" stroke produces the elevation needed to clear the net and at the same time gives the ball enough "rub" to create topspin.

If you keep your racket face vertical you'll impart "over spin" (top spin) to the ball, which will

Straight (two parts)   **Round (one part, continuous)**

Making a nice little "C" or going around an imaginary little clock as you make your backswing will produce a continuous motion for your groundies.

help it come down into the court after it has passed over the net. You can keep your racket at the right attitude with different grips. Think of the forehand drive as if the palm of your hand is hitting the ball. Then if you place your hand on the handle so your racket isn't leaning back or forward too far, you'll have a forehand grip that's comfortable for you. One way to acquire a good "eastern forehand" grip is to hold the racket at its throat with your non-playing hand. Then, with the racket head held vertically, place your playing hand on the strings. Now draw your playing hand down to the grip and shake hands with it. You'll have an eastern forehand grip and can modify it to suit your liking.

I want to add here that beginning players do not have to worry about spin. Good, solid contact with the ball that is played comfortably over the net at slower speeds as recommended in the SAS section is all you need to do. As you begin to hit harder spin becomes more important. So don't try to impart lots of spin to your forehand if you're new to the game.

I mentioned earlier that, once the ball leaves the racket, turning the face of the racket over has no effect. Turning the racket face over after the ball is gone is like a golfer arching his/her back after putting. If the putt isn't on line arching one's back isn't going to drop the putt. And, once the ball has left the racket, turning the head of the racket over can't possibly spin or change it. It's important to understand that it's what you do before you meet the ball that counts. The important part of the swing is from the end of the back swing to the point of contact, not from the point of contact to the end of the follow through. If you have your back swing below the point of contact and are hitting forward and up through the contact area to a high follow-through you'll be in the proper stroke plane when you hit a forehand drive. Your follow through will be just about right too, if you "catch the racket" with your other hand as you finish the stroke. This brings you right back to a good ready position with both hands on the racket.

The end of one's follow through may vary with each player which is okay, as long as you "hit through the ball" at the contact area. I like to have beginning and intermediate players start their stroke with a slightly bent elbow and finish with the arm extended. The elbow and wrist are slightly bent in the ready position so they can remain this way until the arm extends from contact into follow-through. Most beginning and intermediate players who bend their elbow following-through over their shoulder don't stay in the contact area long enough to hit "through the ball" properly. You can correct this mistake by imagining that you have to hit the ball twice in the contact area. Or you can think of your racket head as a pipe that you must make the ball go through. This helps you stay with the shot longer so that you don't pull your racket away from ball contact too soon. When you begin to hit forehands harder you'll need more spin. Then you might want to shift your grip farther under the handle and start your swing a little lower, so the upward motion will make you follow-through over your shoulder. Keeping "your head on the ball" helps you stay with the shot longer with any follow-through.

When you hit a closed stance forehand drive, your goal should be to start early enough so that, by the time you have turned, made your back swing, and come forward, you will meet the ball in front, before it passes your front leg. As you lean into the shot and lift your stroke through the contact point you'll transfer your weight and apply topspin at the same time. Finding this combination gives one a satisfying feeling when hitting a forehand drive. All your shots may not go in but you'll be able to make minor corrections because you understand the stroke fundamentals. When you use an open stance you can't hit the ball quite as far forward. You must not let it get too far behind, however, or you'll lose all your weight transfer power.

• BACKHAND – I want to speak first about the one-hand backhand. Since I've been explaining forehand fundamentals, I can truly say that everything that's been said about forehand technique applies to the backhand too, with one exception, the grip.

Before I go further I want to explain that hitting the ball "out front" dictates how you must grip the racket for your one-hand backhand. If you can picture meeting the ball on your backhand side, slightly forward of your front leg, you've located the "out front" spot for ball contact. Try holding your racket head vertically with a forehand grip to do this. It's very uncomfortable. Your wrist rolls out in front of your grip into a very weak position. However, if you put the palm of your hand on top of the handle you can easily hold the racket in a vertical position.

Obviously, you must change your grip to hit your one-handed backhand. Remember that when you drive the ball from the backcourt you want to hit from low to high to clear the net and impart topspin to the ball. It's impossible to do this with a forehand grip. It doesn't work either when you only change your grip slightly toward a backhand grip. Your forehand grip holds the racket handle on the side, which simulates using the palm of your hand. To properly hit your backhand, you can't keep it in this position. Prove this to yourself by taking a backhand grip and imagine hitting a forehand with it. That wouldn't work either.

Another way to locate a backhand grip is to stand next to a table and put your hand down flat on it. Notice how your wrist bends to do this. Now imagine the top of your racket handle as a tabletop and put your hand on it the same way. Close your fingers around the handle and you'll be ready to hit a backhand "out in front" with a lifted stroke. If you don't have this "kink" in your wrist you will not have the strength to lift the stroke properly.

There's more difference to the backhand grip than just turning it from the side to the top of the handle. I discovered this when I was playing the tennis circuit some years ago. The difference is that in order to pull up under the ball like you do with a forehand, you must have your fingers under the handle like you do for a forehand. To do this you can't have your forefinger spread like you do for a forehand. You must bring your fingers together in a "hammer" grip. You'll be amazed how much stronger you feel hitting your backhand with this grip. Now the racket won't pull out of your hand when you lift through the shot. This is why two-handed backhands are easy to hit with topspin. There are two hands under the racket handle to pull the racket up from low to high to give the ball a good topspin "rub."

The reason that most people only "chip" their backhands is that they have never properly made the grip change. One of the reasons they haven't is that they do not have both hands on the racket in the ready position. If you're right-handed it's your left hand that makes it possible to change your grip. With your left fingers at the throat of the racket holding the

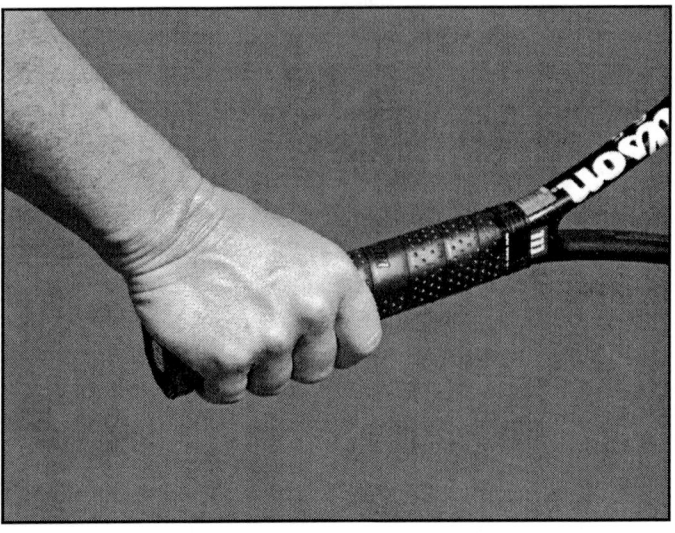

A good one hand backhand grip will make your wrist "kink" a little. That's okay, it shows that you have turned away from the forehand grip properly.

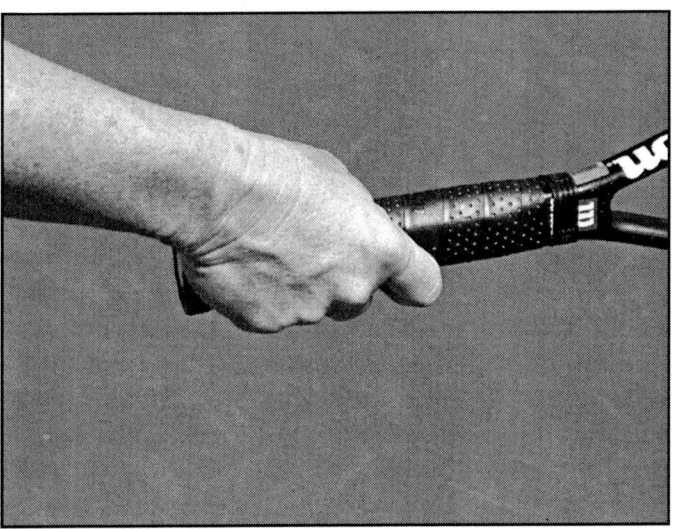

There's no "kink" in your wrist when you haven't made enough turn for your backhand grip.

racket head in a vertical position as you take the racket back, it's easy to move a quarter of a turn from the side to the top of the grip. It's really easy when you point the head of the racket at the fence behind you. With the racket handle level the logo on the butt of the racket then points at the ball and you can easily find the grip. You can practice taking your racket back and changing your grip at home in front of a mirror. The move becomes automatic and takes no longer to change than not to change. You can still "chip" the ball with this grip and it makes high backhands easier to hit too. You will really feel that you're behind the shot, not pulling it.

Speaking of the "chip," it's a shot that every player needs. If I had my choice and could only have either a drive or a chip, I'd take the chip. It's so very versatile. It's probably an easier shot to learn for most people than the drive.

"Chipping" or "slicing" the ball puts underspin on it. This is a stroke that is hit opposite to the way that one hits a drive. You hit from high to low on this one. It's best to hit this shot from a closed backhand stance. You must also hit through the ball with your racket face slightly open. You won't get a good result if you only chop down on it.

The backhand chip or slice shot can be used to return serve and make coming in shots, lobs, and drop shots. It's especially handy if you're late getting in position. It can be hit farther back behind you than a drive. Backhand drives should be hit when you've got the ball right where you want it. Chip shots are necessary to round out the repertoire of both one and two-hand backhand players.

• BACKHANDS AND FOREHANDS USING BOTH HANDS – These are strokes that are quite common among today's players. However, there have been players of other eras who used two hands for their groundstrokes as well. My good friend and UCLA teammate, Ron Livingston, had great success playing two hands for both forehand and backhand. Ron was a NCAA singles finalist and won the doubles with Bob Perry, another teammate of mine.

Many players begin as children using two hands for both shots. They continue to use two hands for backhands as they mature, which is fine. One exception to this is Pete Sampras who started off as a youth using two hands but then switched to a one-hand backhand. As great a player as he became, I really believe that if he had kept his two-hand backhand, he might have become even more successful. He would have had to learn a one-hand backhand as well in order to have all of the tools for championship play. But I believe that he would have had a better shot at the French Open and been more successful on clay if he had kept his two-hand shot. That's mere speculation on my part, of course.

I think the reason that pros teach children to play with both hands is that they really don't understand the "out front" basic that is so important for one-hand backhands. If this basic is not taught and understood, hitting the backhand with one hand is especially difficult. When a ball gets past a certain point it becomes impossible to drive it with a lifted, one hand, topspin stroke. My honest opinion is that a two-handed backhand, if you're right handed, is basically a supported left-hand forehand. The left hand plays a very dominant role when making this shot. If you are left-handed the opposite is true.

I have successfully taught many children and adults a one-hand backhand. Students need to know, by demonstration, where "out front" is. Ball contact has to be made before the ball passes your front leg, while you are in a side-ways stance. When you hit a one-hand backhand with a closed stance your shoulder is on the front side of your body. So, if you meet the ball early the shot just flows freely. I truly believe that because of this it's an easier, more natural shot than the forehand.

It's when the ball gets too far behind that the one-hand backhand needs another hand to help. You must either use the other hand or "chip" it with one hand. Learning a two-hand backhand will give you a very powerful, versatile shot. I also feel that for the best combination two-hand grip, two handers should change their lower hand, at least slightly, toward the one- hand

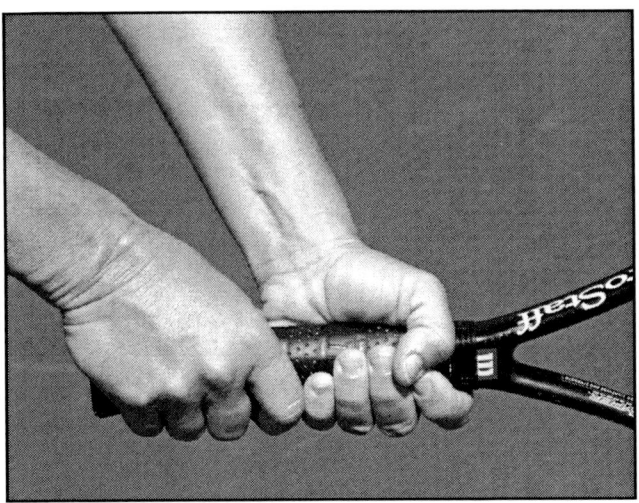

Turning your dominant hand toward the backhand grip will make it easier to "chip" the ball if you have to.

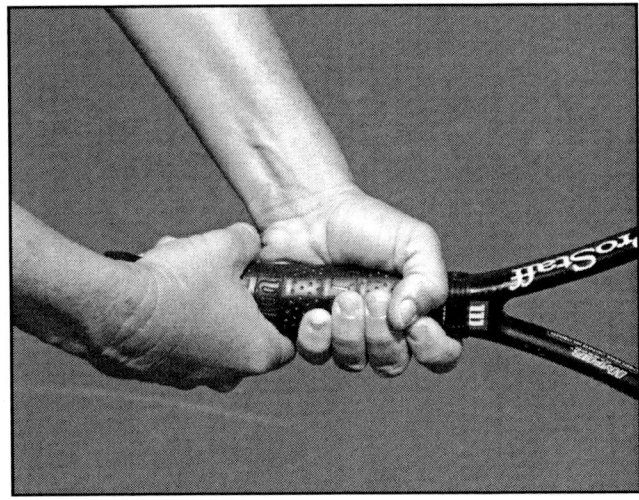

Some players prefer not to change so much, so they can point the racket head back farther in the backswing.

backhand position. Then, when they need to execute a one-hand shot, they'll be ready for it.

There are a number of reasons that a two-handed backhand works so well. The first is the solid feeling of the ball on contact. Both hands control the racket head better, especially with miss hits. Second, the quicker, shorter stroke works so well when returning serves. Third, the quickness to change shot directions is very deceptive. And fourth, using two hands makes a player use the strong muscles of the upper body to add power to the shots. Players using two hands can hit over higher backhands as well. One-handers have to slice or chip these higher bouncing shots.

My advice here is that if you can, use both hands on your backhand, but learn to hit with one hand too. You're going to need both as you reach higher levels of play. Plus, you need one-handed confidence if you want to volley properly. You're going to need this shot if you play doubles often.

I just want to touch on the two-handed forehand. It's not used nearly as much as the two-handed backhand. Most players want to hit with one hand for this shot.

The grips for the one-handed forehand have changed dramatically from former days when hard courts were slicker, balls bounced faster and lower, and grass court play was more popular. The slower courts of today produce higher bounces and the stiff, high-energy light rackets have combined to force many better players to use a "western" grip. With this grip your palm is moved about a quarter turn so that it's under the grip rather than placed on the grip's side. The combination of new rackets and this "western" grip can produce incredibly powerful forehand drives with one hand.

Consequently, using two hands for a forehand isn't really much help. Players can "do it all" with one hand. And using a "western" grip with two hands on the racket handle doesn't fit very well either. This two-hand style for your forehand is not something I recommend.

• SERVE – Most players would agree that this is the most important shot in tennis. I have a feeling that the service return, always rated the second most important shot, is creeping up on the serve in importance. I'll leave this debate for you and your friends to decide.

One thing not debatable is the primary importance of the second serve. Trust me. It's more important than your first serve. There are several good reasons for this. Not the least of them is that "double faults" will plague you if you don't have a reliable second serve. As you grow in the game you will find many other reasons to cultivate a good second serve. Remember when I told you that the only way to "fly" was by SAS? And then in Phase Four, how I explained "Percentage Tennis?" You have already read, hopefully, how understanding these and other basics dictates so much when you are learning and/or correcting strokes. Now let's see how they apply to the serve.

First, in serving as with the other strokes, you have to get the ball over that barrier, the net. You have to give yourself margin for error too, as much as 4 to 5 feet of clearance. Now I suppose you'll think if you do this and hit the serve with any pace at all the ball will never come down in the service box. And of course it won't unless you put some topspin on it. That's what you needed to do for your ground strokes too, wasn't it? But wait a minute. Didn't SAS dictate that at first you should hit the ball safely and also slower if necessary, to play percentage tennis? So, let's add speed and topspin to the serve after we're able to play it safely and accurately.

When I start little kids learning to serve they learn to hit "rainbows." Younger ones stand closer to the net so they're not too far away. But I like everyone who is just learning to serve to hit "rainbows" at first. When they do this they get the first feeling of hitting up at the ball on serve. Most students can do this easily with a perfectly flat grip. You can get this grip by putting your racket on the court and just picking it up by the handle. Hitting "rainbows" gives you clearance or margin for error over the net and a correct mental picture of the serve.

It's amazing but so many people have an opposite image of what to do for a serve. They think they've seen good players toss the ball up so they could hit down at the ball to get it into the service court. So they toss the ball up in order to hit it down. Wrong. That may appear to be what good servers are doing, but no, they're not doing that at all. There is no way players can put topspin on their serve if they do that. Actually hitting down produces underspin, which is the opposite of what is needed. Good players hit up at the ball very vigorously to be able to clear the net and bring the ball down into the service court. This can't be done with the flat grip I've just described. A service grip must be used to hit the ball a glancing, upward blow to impart topspin. Doesn't this remind you of what was required when you hit groundstrokes? But more on this grip later.

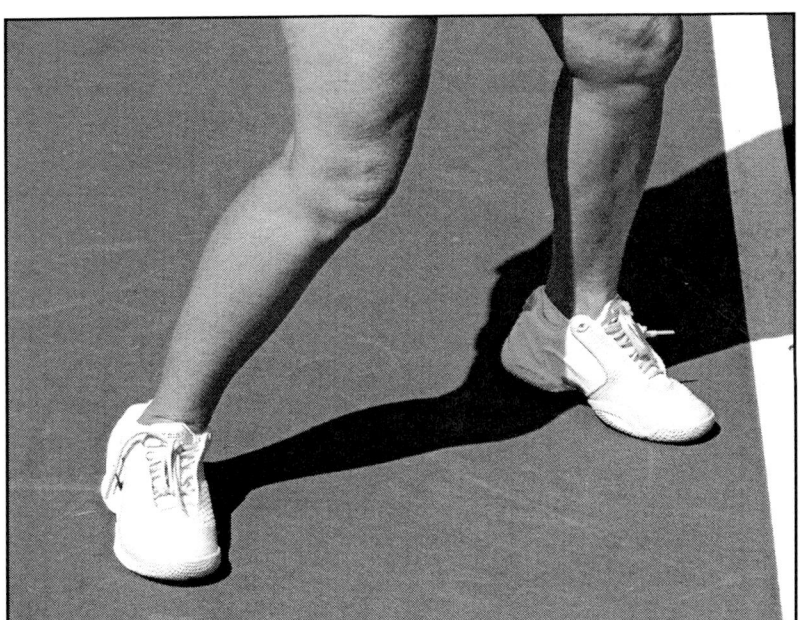

When you line up to serve you need to be standing sideways to the direction you're aiming. You need to do this so you can get some weight transfer the same as for your other shots. Your front foot should be about 3 to 4 inches behind the base line, with your back foot lined up shoulder-width behind it. If you imagine a line through both feet pointing toward the direction of your serve, you'll have your feet placed correctly. Pointing your front foot at a slight angle toward the baseline will make it easier to follow through.

If you draw an imaginary line through your two feet it will point toward the court you are serving into. Use this method for setting your stance on the ad court as well.

You should hold the ball in the fingers and thumb of your non-playing hand. When you turn your hand over the ball should not drop out. Place the ball on the strings or under the throat of the racket for a good ready position. Don't touch or hold the racket with the fingers holding the ball.

When you are learning you should spend some time practicing your toss. You want the ball out in front of your forward foot and tossed high enough so that you need to stretch some to hit it. A good practice to learn to toss the ball is to stand facing sideways to the fence, about 3 feet away. Reach up as high as you can on tiptoes to see how high your toss should be. Then place your racket flat on the court with the head in front of your forward foot. Now hold the ball directly over the racket head about waist high. Keep your palm up. Just make a 1–2 motion, down and up and release the ball. If you do this properly you'll be able to see the ball's seams, because it shouldn't turn much with a good release. When you toss the ball to the right height and direction it will come down and bounce off your strings. If the ball touches the fence you tossed it too far forward. If it bounces behind you, obviously you tossed it too far back. Make sure, as well, that your ball goes high enough each time. You need to practice this until you can make the ball bounce off your strings most of the time.

When you begin your serve, from your ready position, both hands will be in action. This is sometimes difficult. I use a rhythm system which may be described as, "Up together, down and split apart." Both hands rise up slightly before dropping and splitting. One hand can then go back up with the ball toss while the other makes the service motion with the racket. At first it helps to practice this without holding a ball, just to get the feeling of the "up

All of your fingers should be touching the ball for good preparation to make your service toss.

If you have to "re-grab" the ball as you start your toss, you won't be as consistently accurate with your toss.

together, down and split apart." It's a good practice to do this off court to train beginners.

Try to "roll" your wrist and hand over when you finish your follow-through on the opposite side of your body. This "pronation" will help to keep you from hitting your shins in the follow through, as mentioned in the "staying healthy" section of Sound Fundamentals in Phase Four. The service motion should be just like throwing a ball.

The timing of this should be such that the service motion accelerates your racket up to its contact with the ball. A slow, relaxed start helps you to do this. If you soften your grip and wrist and just make a throwing motion with the racket it will flow quite easily. (Your grip automatically tightens as you reach for the ball.) In serving acceleration is an important constant, just like your footing. What I mean by this is that you shouldn't change either of them to adjust for the toss. Many players move their front foot when going after a poor toss. Others stop their acceleration to correct for tosses that are too high. They get what is called a "hitch" in their serve.

The serve is the only stroke you can practice by yourself. All you need is a bucket of balls and an empty court. Just remember the main parts of the serve: stance, accelerated motion and ball toss. The first two are constants. It's the toss that's the variable. Don't "go fishing" for a bad toss by moving your front foot. And don't "hitch" your motion if you toss too high. Adjust your toss to fit these other two fundamentals.

I said earlier that I would talk about the grip you'll need to impart topspin to your serve. It's actually a grip

Check the height for your toss on the fence. It's okay if you toss a little higher than you can reach.

Start your toss directly over your racket, and then try to toss to the right height and make the ball bounce on your racket strings.

that is half way between your forehand and backhand grips, the same as your volley grip. When you use this grip for the first time you're going to hit a lot of serves down and to the left, if you are right-handed. That's fine. You need to counter this by aiming much higher and much farther to the right than you think you should. Do this and now you'll be hitting up at the ball on serve applying topspin. At first it's an amazing feeling. You can hardly believe that it works. Your "rainbow" serve can now be hit much harder and the ball won't go

When you throw a ball your hand pronates as shown.

When you finish your serve, which is basically a throwing motion, pronate the racket just the same.

If you don't pronate you might hit your shin, ouch!

out. It's simply amazing. Lots of repetition is what is needed now. You've learned to hit a reliable second serve. I'd advise a few lessons to learn variations of spin and flat, hard serves. You're going to have more confidence to try these because you can always go back to your reliable second serve.

I want to make a final point here about all of these strokes. Please notice that with each of them I've insisted they be hit "out in front." The one exception is the "chip" or "sliced" backhand, which can be hit farther back when necessary. The similarity then for forehands, backhands, and serves is that you're leaning forward and lifting or hitting up when you hit the ball. When you hit volleys and chips "out in front" you'll also be leaning in but hitting from high to low. Timely "leaning in" makes your weight transfer into the shot. When this valuable lever is applied you can hit with plenty of power with very little strain on your body. This is certainly a definite plus but not the only one.

When using all available levers a player may stroke more slowly and still hit what's called a "heavy ball." You'll actually get more on your shots with less effort than players who flail away with fast, wild swings and no weight transfer. Moreover, you'll control your shots better with a slower swing. Your percentages will go up. You'll be like a baseball player with a high batting average who hits singles most of the time. Let the home run hitters enjoy themselves. You'll be the one still standing at the end of the match.

CORRECTING YOUR STROKES – You're the coach.

You have to be. The reality is that no one else, especially your opponent, is going to help you. When you're out there, perhaps in the middle of a point, you will sometimes have to change or modify things quickly. Sometimes you'll be to late for that point but if you figure out what you need, you can correct for the next one. I'll be talking here about adjustments in your mechanics, not in your tactics or strategy.

The key for correcting your strokes is to know your basics and be able to recognize when you may have forgotten something you should be doing. There are a number of "tell tale" clues that will remind you to correct certain things. The list below will give you a few of them. You'll discover some of your own too.

- Your groundstrokes are clearing the net okay but continue to carry too long. This probably means that your racket head is leaning back too far at impact. Change your grip a little to close the racket face. This happens often on backhands when players don't change their backhand grip enough. Or maybe getting under the ball more on your back swing so you can hit with more "under – up" motion will help. You might need to follow through higher as well. You need to find the balance between power and spin to control the shot. Still keep your "margin for error" clearance. You don't want to change that.

- Your groundstrokes are not clearing the net, creating too many "bad" errors. Most of the time in this case your grip is probably okay. You just need to aim your shot higher over the net. More "margin" is needed here.

- Your groundies are going cross-court okay but when you hit down the line they're going wide all the time. Players naturally tend to hit "around the outside" of cross-court shots. When they try down the line shots they tend to hit too much behind or inside the ball. This gives the ball a curve that carries it wide. Get around those down the liners too.

- Your elbow hurts when you hit your one-hand backhand. I already mentioned this in Phase Four but it's worth mentioning here again. You're not hitting the ball "out in front" enough. And you're probably not changing to a full backhand grip so you can be behind the shot. Use both hands to make the grip change and start earlier. Even if you are chipping or slicing the ball you'll need to hit it sooner. Elbow pain is usually on the outside of your elbow joint. Get ready earlier, make a full grip change and you'll be meeting the ball "out in front" where you want it.

- Your serves continue to go long – you're tossing the ball too far back. Your serves continue to go into the net – you're tossing the ball too far forward. When you are looking up at your toss while serving it's sometimes hard to know if your toss is in the right place. The clues of where your shots are going tell you how to correct.

- You can't seem to get enough topspin on your serve to bring it down into the service court. You are brushing up on the ball but something is wrong. Lots of players start their serve with a good grip in the ready position but don't realize that they are changing it toward the forehand side in the middle of their motion. It often takes a few buckets of practice serves to overcome this bad habit. If you take your proper grip, hold it throughout the serve but it feels funny, you've probably been changing your grip while you serve.

- You are holding your grip throughout the serve but they still aren't going in. In this case a couple of things may be wrong. The first one is that you're not keeping your head up looking at the ball when you make contact. Pulling your head down too soon is a common error with many players' serves. The second problem may be that you are not relaxed enough with your wrist to allow the racket to "scratch your back" during the swing. Keep in mind that the important part of the service motion is from the bottom of the "back scratch" to the point of contact. That's the real part of the motion that goes up to the ball to make topspin. When you don't have enough "back scratch" it's like not getting any "under-up" in your groundstrokes. When you serve it should feel like you're hitting right up into the sky. Rod Laver used to say that when he was serving his best, even on hard ace serves, he felt like the ball left his racket going up. I really liked that. He was doing a "Laver rainbow." Before I forget it, I must tell you that a common cause of not being able to "scratch your back" enough is that you're dropping your elbow. Keep it up as you lift your racket behind you. Then if your wrist is relaxed your racket can drop behind your back properly.

- Tendonitis can develop in your shoulder too, if you're too stiff in your service motion. A stiff swing and ball toss that's too far back is a bad combination. Players who do this look like they're throwing a hand grenade when they serve. This is generally a difficult dual problem to overcome. Most players who do this probably haven't ever thrown a ball much. They just don't have a smooth throwing motion. Years ago, when the great Grand Slam champion Maureen Connolly was having trouble with her serve, her coach Teach Tennant, took her out to Balboa Park in San Deigo for a unique practice. Coach Tennant, as the story goes, brought some old rackets for Maureen to throw. The coach found a grassy area where they could throw the rackets back and forth to each other. She did this to help Maureen find a better throwing motion for her serve. You could do the same by throwing footballs or softballs with a friend or someone in your family. If you throw right-handed you should serve right-handed and the same goes for left-handers. And don't forget to keep your toss out in front.

- If your volleys are going astray or you're miss hitting them you could have two problems. Not being able to "punch" them in the direction you want may be because you're swinging too much. Both lateral and vertical direction should be easy to control if you are "blocking or punching" your volley. Squeezing your grip can help to firm up your wrist just as you make contact. Any "flopping" of the racket head after contact really fouls things up. Letting the ball get too far behind the right "out front" point of contact often causes miss hits. When you meet the ball behind this point you can't follow it to the strings. Meeting the ball as far in front as you can comfortably do it never hurts. Stay out in front of the "glass wall" I described in "Understanding the Strokes." You'll get great contact and be able to see the court and the ball. You'll be able to direct it where you want it when you block or punch it "out in front."

- When you miss opportunities with your overhead smash by continually hitting out, what should you do? Well, first you should think of what you do on your serve when it sails too far. Remember, with that one your ball toss was too far behind you. Same thing here. Except you aren't the one who put the ball up there in the wrong place. What you have done is not get ready early enough so you could get back under it properly. Either that or you just misjudged where you needed to be. You may have taken a big service type of swing. That would take longer and cause a late hit. The answer is to shorten your take-a-way motion from your ready position. Just lift your racket over your shoulder as you slide back with a side step. When a lob goes up it's better to be too far back than not back far enough. You can always move forward. You can meet the ball farther forward on an overhead than you do on a serve. Also, you shouldn't hurry to hit your overhead smash on a high defensive lob. The timing is very difficult when the ball is coming straight down. Let these high ones bounce and they will be much easier to put away. Start early, get well behind it with your racket over your shoulder, meet it well out in front, flatten your racket face a bit, and mush it into your opponents court for a winner. Wow, that feels good!

These nine examples are only the tip of the iceberg of errors that you can correct with your own coaching. Knowledge of basic fundamentals is the key, which helps you make these corrections. Players at all levels need fine tuning once in a while. Tennis is, indeed, a "thinking person's game," both for the mechanics of stroking as well as for tactics and strategy.

My final piece of advice for correcting your errant strokes is this. Most players have a favorite stroke or strokes. They also have a weaker one. Whether it's your strength or weakness, there are days when things aren't going so well. We all tend to get a little tentative when this happens. It's perfectly natural. Looking up too early on groundstrokes, pulling your head down on serves, not hitting through, and leaning back when you hit are all signs of being tentative. What you have to do here is "trust your strokes." You must stay positive and aggressively hit your shots. You may miss a few, and lose a few points while you're getting back in the groove but go ahead and keep your head on the ball and hit your shots. Don't baby them. Direct your shots down the middle for a while to give yourself plenty of margin. Give yourself big targets. Get that good "leaning in and lifting up" feeling by hitting your groundies out in front. Or keep tossing out front for serves and vigorously hit up with your head on the ball. Fundamentals, fundamentals, fundamentals are your saving grace.

COMPETITIVE DRILLS – Purposeful, quality workouts

Hitting thousands of balls will make a player out of you. The real questions are how long will it take and how effective is your practice? Rallying with another player, hitting against a wall and using a ball machine are conventional methods most players use to work on their games. I'm not going to discourage you from doing these workouts, but I have a more excellent way to practice that will help you reach higher levels of play more quickly.

The drills I'm going to suggest combine the repetition of the conventional methods, mentioned above, with an element of competition. The competitive element is the key to quality practice. When there is no element of competition too many shots are wasted in unnecessary errors. Practicing should focus on eliminating errors as much as possible. And the drills will simulate what really goes on during match play. You need to be fundamentally sound with your strokes to be able to do these drills.

- The first one I call my "UCLA" drill. My coach JD Morgan, who later became UCLA's Athletic Director, was a real taskmaster. He developed a drill that simulates a passing shot situation. The coach sets up, with a basket of balls, in the center of one service court. The player starts from a center ready position behind the baseline. Let's say we want to practice the backhand pass down the line. The coach hits the ball to the player's forehand. Player then hits a medium hard shot back to the coach, who volleys the ball to the backhand. Player runs to hit the pass down the line. Immediately the coach hits another ball to the forehand and volleys player's return to the backhand for another pass down the line. The aerobics and making the pass into the court make for a very high quality workout. This drill is not for beginners. Players need to have pretty good skills before they can do this one. You can imagine four different ways to do this drill so both crosscourt and down the line passes can be worked on for both forehand and backhand.

This "UCLA" drill is a very aerobic workout for players capable of doing it. It's a great passing shot practice.

• The next drill focuses on the overhead and recovery volley. This is excellent training because it's what you should do in either a singles or doubles situation. Here's how it works. One player is stationed at the net and the other at the baseline. The baseline player can be positioned in the center, the backhand, or the forehand corners. The baseline player starts the rally with a groundstroke to the net person. Net person volleys back and baseline person lobs. Net person hits an overhead back to the baseliner who hits it as short as possible. The net person has to hit the volley before it bounces. Then the baseliner hits another lob. When the net player hits the overhead he/she must recover in time to get the short return before it hits the ground. This drill also is not for beginners. It's very aerobic and teaches the net player to hustle back into position after hitting the overhead. It's a good practice for the baseliner too, requiring a soft touch to lob and hit short. I call this game "no bounce."

"No bounce" is also a very aerobic drill that simulates getting back for your overhead and then making your recovery volley.

As soon as she volleys back to me I'm going to lob again.

"Up and back" stresses depth over direction for both players.

- When I was playing the circuit the great Harry Hopman was coach of the Australian Davis Cup team. I got to know him and practiced some with him myself. He showed me the following drill that he often used to train his team. This drill is played in only half of the court – either "straight ahead" or "catty-corner" – and within the singles lines. (You have to imagine an extension of the center service line.) One player plays the backcourt and the other at net. Either player can start the rally but the points don't start until the backcourt player gets the second shot in play. After that the point begins. Since the direction is pretty much set, it's the depth of both players' shots that sets up a winner. The net player's volley depth keeps the backcourt player at bay. And the backcourt player's lobs, short shots, and hard drives challenge the net player. Drop volleys often win points. And if the backcourt player gets a good lob over the net player, he/she can take the net away and gain that advantage. I like to play until one of the players gets five points. If the game is tied at four all you have to win by two points. I call this game "up and back."

- The next drill I call "threes." One of the players either reaches negative three or positive three to end the game. Here's how to play. Both players start from the backcourt. One player begins the rally and both players have to hit the ball into play twice before the point begins. Once the point starts it's played out just the same as you would in a real game. A clean winner gives a player one point. Any errors cost minus one-half point. So if you make a clean winner you earn one point. Then on the next rally if you make an error you lose one half point, so now you only have plus one-half, and so on. You'll be amazed how long it takes either player just to get to positive or negative three. It's okay to come to the net if you get an opportunity. Drop shots or any ploy is permitted just as they would be in a game. My son Jim, is a 5.5 NTRP player so he gives me the doubles lines in this drill. Any better player can still get a good workout with a lesser player by doing this.

- My next drill is for practicing your serve under pressure. You'll need a basket of balls for this one. After you do some warm up serves you can begin to test yourself with this drill. Set a goal of getting five serves in a row into the service court. When you get four in a row the fifth one gets a little tough to make. If you miss anywhere before your five in a row you have to start over. When you can do five, challenge yourself to make ten in a row, then twenty, etc. This practice will help you develop the confidence you'll need at key points in a match. This drill is good for developing a reliable second serve that has a good accelerated service motion. Start adding depth when you can reach numbers goals in this drill. Make yourself hit that fifth one deep as well as in the court. You can also challenge yourself to goals of hitting certain areas of the service court five or more times. "Pressure serving" is the name for this drill.

- I call my next drill "crosscourts." You play to 10 points in this one and both players have to hit everything on their forehands into only half of the singles court. (If a lefty is playing a righty then the righty hits forehands and the lefty hits only backhands.) If, for example, the righty is pulled way out of court on the forehand side and the other player forces the righty to hit a backhand he/she wins a point. Any time a player makes an error the other player gets a point as well. The crosscourt backhand drill works the same way. You have to imagine an extension of the center service line when you play this half-court drill. You'll find that you really have to move your feet to keep hitting forehands. (The same will be true for the crosscourt backhand drill.)

- My final drill called "doubles," is great practice for serving and returning serve in doubles. It also emphasizes the importance of the first volley and moving into net behind your serve or return. You play normal points in half-court crosscourt doubles. Again, imagine a line extended from the center service line to the baseline. One player serves, the other returns. Play best four out of seven point games and then reverse the roles. The importance of first serves and good, low-returns is obvious, just as it is in real competition. This is an especially good warm-up drill before your team plays a tournament match.

Obviously, all of these drills emphasize keeping the ball in play. You can't waste shots or you can't do the drills. And if you're having trouble with certain shots, you can work to make corrections by doing these drills. Quality practice is worth tons more than just hitting balls with no particular thought or purpose. I hope you will try some of these. You'll be practicing your strokes in the same environment as when you're using them in competition. You will have to either work with a pro or a buddy to do them. I'm quite sure you'll be pleased with the results.

PHASE SIX
GROWING IN THE GAME AS A YOUNG PLAYER

WHEN CHILDREN SHOULD START –
Starting at an early age makes tennis easier to learn.

You really can't start them too early if they show an interest. I have pictures of my little grandson Chase Huebner trying to lift his racket to serve when he was only 18 months old. He could imitate what he had seen his dad John Huebner do when he served. Kids have remarkable imitative skills. Chase wasn't really able to hit his serve correctly but I'm sure he thought he was doing it perfectly.

Kids can soak up tennis skills like a sponge when they're young. They have the time as well to get the repetition needed. They're going to do what they see. Visualization and imitation are great ways to learn the strokes.

As a teaching pro for many years, I know how difficult it is for students to translate what's said verbally into the mechanics of stroke making. Just saying, "Do what I do" is much easier. That's where kids have such an advantage.

My grandson Chase really thought he was serving!

Assistant pro, Brian Junio, working with some little guys at the Copper River Country Club tennis facility in Fresno, California.

So my advice is to start your children off as early as possible when they show an interest. Little, light rackets are available, and sponge balls, called "nerf" balls, can hardly cause any damage, even indoors. You can encourage a first fascination for tennis with these little toys.

Actually going out on the court to attempt some shots probably won't happen much before kids are 3 to 4 years old. Taking children out when you practice as a family can increase your their curiosity and interest. However, I don't recommend doing this when you're playing a match with a friend or friends. Kids can be a problem and very annoying to others in this situation.

By 3 or 4, though, some formal training can begin, especially if you have already introduced your kids to the game. You need to check out who is known for being good with little ones and might be available in your area.

I hope you fellows don't get on me for this, but as a head pro I've always felt that the women on my staff did a good job with kids this age. Many female pros have a special way with kids, especially the littlest ones. Kids identify with them easily. Patience and making things fun are very important for these first tennis experiences. A good pro needs to have these qualities to do an excellent job with these little tennis players.

Group lessons of 3 or 4 students and clinics of 5 to 6 kids are fine for starters. More students than this make it too difficult to keep kids controlled and all doing something to keep busy.

It's great when moms or dads want to stay during the lesson. Most pros like this because then parents learn too. They can take this learning away and use it to help outside the lesson time. I previously alluded to the importance of parental help in Phase Three under the "Parents are necessary for kids" heading. As much as pros want their students to improve, they can't be as effective without parental help.

At ages 3 and 4, kids can practice at home, you don't have to go out to the courts every time. Doing bouncing drills and hitting against garage doors often helps to improve hand-eye skills. Kids at this age may even take their rackets to bed. Pros want kids to treat their rackets like a friend, so this bonds them with their racket. As they grow in the game their racket needs to become a part of them.

When children reach the ages of 5, 6 and 7, their motor skills really start to click in and their attention spans get longer. They can do a lot more at these ages. If they haven't started a tennis program it's still plenty early to start. It's interesting to note that most world class players started playing when they were very young. I'm frequently amazed at how well some children play by the time they're in Middle School grades. They couldn't get that good without starting years earlier.

These young players are often outstanding students in school. I think the discipline required to get top grades in school transfers over to their tennis games. Commitment is required to gain study discipline. Tennis requires this same kind of discipline. Commitment to learning tennis for children and adults has been pointed out earlier in Phase Three. And I really encourage all my young tennis students to excel in school. When they do their tennis benefits too.

Starting to play and take lessons when children get to the 8 to 12 year ages is still a great time to begin. They still have the ability to "see and do." And, tennis has great social value at this age. Children have a lot of fun with their friends in the clinics or group lessons. I want to pause at this point to say that regardless of when kids start to learn tennis, their first order of priority should be the same. It should be to learn tennis as a lifetime sport. Just the enjoyment of playing should never be lost. Unfortunately, it can be lost when winning, rankings, scholarships, and money overwhelm the fun of playing. Sometimes a reminder about why we play the game keeps us on track. I really think players play better when they don't lose the fun of the game.

TENNIS MOMS AND DADS – How to be one.

I've been there, done that. I made some mistakes too. But I think I learned fairly quickly when I did goof up. I'm going to do my best to pass on what I've learned from my own experiences and from what I've seen and heard over the years.

Our oldest boy Jim, was highly ranked in boy's 14's in Northern California. One day he told me he wanted to quit tennis and go out for his high school cross-country team. I must say I was really taken aback. Without realizing it I was already looking ahead to his playing at much higher levels. But I quickly came to my senses and told him if that's what he wanted to do I would support him wholeheartedly. He went on to be a fine middle distance runner and earned a college track scholarship. The end of the story is that he's a family man now and greatly enjoying his tennis again.

Gretchen's and my other two children, John and Karin, both went on to college with scholarships after their junior tennis. They're both still involved in tennis coaching. John is Tennis Director at the Silver Creek Valley Country Club in San Jose, California. Karin has been the assistant coach for the women's tennis team at the University of Southern California while she pursues her doctorate degree in history.

Gretchen and I covered most of the bases involved in being "tennis mom and dad" for our three children. We must have done some things right during this time because we maintained our loving relationship with all three kids. You can do the same if you keep things in perspective and don't allow the game to get the upper hand.

If your kids play tennis on a just for fun basis your job as a tennis mom or dad will be relatively uncomplicated. You take them to and pick them up from lessons. You pay for lessons, shoes, clothing, rackets and miscellaneous equipment. You help them line up practice games. These are pretty mundane responsibilities. They're not much different from other activities in which your kids participate.

But now suppose your child has become a better than average player. He or she wants to make the high school team, play in tournaments, and even get ranked. Whoa, this means you're going to be a "tennis mom" or "tennis dad." What do you do now?

You know how a rug is supposed to enhance a room but hardly be noticed? You've got it. You're going to be a perfect tennis parent if you do the "rug" thing.
This can be so difficult to do. Here are some of the dos and don'ts in a nutshell:

- Do remember to help your child get their tournament entry in on time.
- Do help them get organized and prepared before match time.
- Do teach your kids good sportsmanship.
- Do remember good sportsmanship yourself. Walk the walk.
- Do let your child keep his/her own score.
- Do affirm your child whether he/she wins or loses.
- Do let your child deal with his/her coach's decisions.
- Do help your child with tennis problems. Work together as a team.
- Do attend as many of your child's matches as you can.
- Do help your child keep tennis in the proper perspective in life.

- Don't make expectations for your child's performance too high.
- Don't push him/her to play tennis if he/she is not interested.
- Don't allow tantrums at any time. Self-control is mandatory.
- Don't allow racket, ball, or verbal abuse.
- Don't ever interfere with line calls in your child's match.
- Don't ever get involved in a scoring dispute. Let an umpire settle it.
- Don't talk loudly or make gestures while watching play.
- Don't talk about opponent's shortcomings to other parents.
- Don't complain about the draw and seeding.
- Don't get into arguments with other parents.

Listing these dos and don'ts is kind of a futile exercise. There's so much more to being a good tennis parent. You and your child are a team. You each have a job to do. Your job is to help your child play his/her very best. The child needs your support for so many things.

Some kids need more than others, of course. It's a balance between "being there" and "not being there." You'll be the best judge of that. But you can be sure that the qualities developed in tennis can be wonderfully applied to all areas of life.

I have to tell you a couple of little stories about when Gretchen's and my kids played junior tournaments. In those days tournaments would provide housing to the players, so it gave kids a chance to meet other families and demonstrate their proper behavior. One time a parent who housed one of our boys said that he told her he never took a shower because it made him weak and affected his tennis. Another young boy who stayed with us during a Fresno tournament stated that, "I never eat anything but steak for dinner." Gretchen was fixing spaghetti that night so she told him frankly, that was all he was going to get. One other parent was very complimentary about the way one of our sons was so neat, had his bed made up and kept everything so organized. We were amazed by this compliment but proud just the same. These youngsters were 10 to 12 year-olds at the time and these experiences were a great part of their tennis growing up.

Gretchen and I had another "mom and dad experience" which has been a life long pleasure. When I was playing the amateur circuit years ago I became very friendly with the then captain of the Japanese Davis Cup Team, Ichiya Kumagae. Ichiya had been one of the world's top players during the Big Bill Tilden-Little Bill Johnson era. He was also a greatly esteemed athlete in Japan and was chosen by the Japan Lawn Tennis Association to lead their Davis Cup team. When I was in the Navy my ship went to Japan and I was able to connect up with "Ichi" for some play with him and his team at the Tokyo Lawn Tennis Club. When "Ichi" passed away a few years after I met him in Japan, Gretchen and I wanted to memorialize him with an offer to take two Japanese junior players under our wing for summer tournaments in California. The Japan Lawn Tennis Association accepted our offer and sent two girls, Naoko "Nana" Sato and Eri Murata, to be our guests for the summer. We knew that the good competition in Northern California junior tournaments would help the Japanese girls improve. Besides, our own children, Jim, John and Karin, would be going to the tournaments anyway so a couple more players just added to the fun. Both the girls were delightful guests but the best part of this story is that we have continued to communicate with them for over thirty years. Both have married. Eri has continued to play competitively as a top player in senior women's tournaments. She and her husband Yoshio, live in a Tokyo suburb. "Nana" has a tennis school in Japan called "Tennis Dream" which she oversees. So they have both kept in touch with the game they love and we feel that they are a part of our own family. We have also kept in touch with Mr. Kumagae's daughter Kazuko, over the years. Obviously, becoming tennis parents can be a most rewarding experience.

You might still be chuckling about my rug example but as a tennis mom or dad if you can enhance your child's tennis and sort of stay in the background so you're not noticed, you'll be doing the "rug" thing as a good tennis parent. Good luck on being a "tennis mom or dad" and learning how to be one.

COMPETITIVE PLAY – Learning to enjoy the challenge.

Billie Jean King was a competitor and a great tennis athlete as well. This combination propelled her to the highest level in tennis. She didn't win all her matches but she was always going to be giving all she had in every match. She had a "love for the struggle," as she aptly put it. The tougher the match became the more she enjoyed it. That's the "competitive greatness" that Coach John Wooden put right at the top of his famous triangle of success. I think Billie Jean was born with this wonderful attribute. But others can learn it. Lot's of people are competitive but can't seem to bring out their best when they want to the most. How can you help your children learn this if they are not already blessed with it?

The first step is to take away the fear of losing. This fear often follows when one's expectations are too high. Coach Wooden had a wonderful saying for his players: "Never think you're better than your opponent, but always think you're just as good." When you start a match with this admonition in mind you're showing respect for your opponent and to yourself as well.

The second step in learning to be at your best in competition is to keep up your intensity and concentration throughout the match. Your mind might want to wander, but if it does, you must take your time and recover the concentration required for what you're doing.

Steadying your emotions is the third thing good competitors do. You cannot do your best when your emotions swing high and low during the course of the match.

The fourth thing good competitors realize is that there are going to be some tough times in every match. You shouldn't be surprised when this happens. You've won the first set but now you're down 4-1 in the second. Did you expect your opponent to fold when you won the first set? Wouldn't you dig down if you lost the first set? When this happens you need to relish the opportunity, not panic or begin to think about losing the set. You're being challenged, so respond with a positive challenge yourself. Be inspired by Billie Jean King and "love the struggle."

My fifth piece of advice for enjoying the challenge of the struggle in a tough match is to keep the match you're playing in perspective. It won't be the last match you will ever play. There will always be other matches, other opportunities, and other challenges. Determine before you start your match that you're going to do everything you can to win but if you don't succeed it won't be the end of the world.

Boris Becker, the great German champion, was once asked after he lost a match how important it was to him. He said, "it was very important but since no one had died or anything like that had happened it couldn't be too much to handle." He could deal with it. I'm paraphrasing what he said here. I think you get the point.

If you make some of these thoughts part of your match preparation I think you'll actually begin to enjoy the challenges presented to you in your matches. You're not going to "beat the challenges" every time but as I said earlier, Billie Jean King didn't win every match either. She enjoyed the "struggle" anyway. You can too.

LEARNING TO WIN – An important part of growing in tennis.

I hope you haven't gotten the idea reading *WHENING* TENNIS that winning has been left out of the picture. Far from it, please. When a match is played someone has to win. It might as well be you. You can't tie a tennis match. What you learn from *WHENING* TENNIS will help you in many ways to close out matches with a victory.

Great players know how to finish. As matches develop you need to keep notes in your head about trends in your opponent's game. When he or she really needed a point what did he/she do best? Also, what have you been doing well? Remembering these things can greatly help ending match strategy.

One other important thing to do is take your time. Players often begin to rush to end a match when they got to the point of winning by being patient and taking their time. Don't change a winning game.

Many players play their best when they're behind in the score. It's natural to want to "hang in there." You've got to realize that near the end of a match you're probably going to have to lift your game. Your opponent is not going to give you the match.

Junior tennis age groups are divided into two-year increments. Some coaches and parents are always entering their students or children in older age groups for experience. I'm not against juniors playing "up" once in a while but some hardly ever play in their own age group. Kids who do this get whipped most of the time and seldom learn to win. Tennis players of all ages need to compete against their contemporaries.

There are also players that won't even practice with players they feel are inferior. This is also a mistake. Lesser players have their "zone" days once in a while just like you do. It's good practice to try to overcome this when someone "zones" on you. There's good reason for this. It might happen to you during tournament play but you'll know what to do if it's happened in practice. Besides if your opponent really isn't as good as you are, you can use the opportunity to practice some of your weaknesses. Virtually any kind of practice can be made valuable.

Also, the most important and sometimes hardest wins come while playing contemporaries. "Playing up" takes the pressure off. If juniors, or adult players for that matter, don't put themselves in the pressure cooker they will never learn to win.

One player who really learned to finish was Andre Agassi. He paid his dues by coming up through the junior ranks. The normal American steps up the junior ladder are to win at home and then on a state and national level. Then many play intercollegiate tennis before entering the professional ranks. When young players have all the talents and desire necessary, it's still their ability to finish - to win - that's going to propel them up to the top.

SETTING GOALS – Make them attainable – but dream a little.

Setting goals is what successful people do. It's true for life, for business and just as true for sports success.

When goals are set they should be made within certain parameters. Setting a time frame is one. Making them reasonable is another. They need to be attainable but allow for improvement to reach a higher level. You will be the best judge of whether your goals are set too high or too low. Cautious optimism is a pretty good mindset for making them.

When world class athletes are interviewed they invariably state that, when they were children, they dreamed of winning a world championship. This is great. It's a distant dream, a goal. It sets up the framework for achieving smaller goals along the way to the top. Most of the world's top tennis players have dreamed as children that they would win a Grand Slam tournament. And many of them use role models as their inspirations. We need to encourage our top athletes to remember their influence on younger generations.

As a tennis player you don't have to aspire to the very top to set goals. Goals should be a part of player's plans at every level. Beginners should reach for intermediate status and intermediates for advanced status, and so forth.

Tennis goals cover basically two areas. The first is to improve fundamentally in the mechanics of the game. The second involves moving up the ladder with more victories.

The first one is really pretty obvious. There are so many different strokes to master that setting goals for better mechanics is never ending. Even after the mechanics have been learned they often slip away and goals need to be set to get them back. But I think that the great majority of players would see great improvement in their victories by merely setting goals to improve their fundamental mechanics. I guess it's like blocking and tackling in football. Or, if you relate better, it's like passing, dribbling, and shooting in basketball. Tennis mechanics include shot placement as well as the "how to" of stroke production. Top players constantly drill certain shots until they feel comfortable. I believe that fundamentals form the framework of every endeavor. Tennis players should be constantly setting goals to improve or fine-tune their fundamental mechanics.

When goals are set for more match victories it gets more difficult. There are innumerable facets for goal setting in this area. I'll take the liberty here to list a few:

- To get in better physical condition: You can't have a more important goal than this for your tennis. Physical condition is the first goal everyone needs to set to play his or her best tennis.

- To gain control of emotions on court: This can be broken down into goals to finish matches better, to not get emotional over bad calls by an opponent, to not fear losing, to not fear winning, and generally to play on as even a keel as possible regardless of the match situation.

- To move up the ladder in ranking or NTRP rating: These are both computer-controlled determinations, which reflect your results in match play. You are not in total control of this. Your opponents will make every effort to deny you this goal. Aspiring young pros set these goals for higher ATP or WTA computer rankings so they can qualify for tournament entry.

- To play well enough to "make the team": Again, this requires winning enough matches to be selected. Maybe going for the junior varsity is the best stepping-stone to begin with. Knowing your competition and being realistic helps set an attainable goal here.

- To receive an athletic scholarship for college: College coaches award tennis scholarships. Coaches have limited scholarships available and want to make every one count. Unfortunately for American juniors, many better foreign players have entered the race for these scholarships. Title Nine has decreased the ones available for men's teams and increased the ones available for women's teams. Players who have a combination of good grades and good rankings have the best chance for tennis scholarships.

- To defeat an opponent who has dominated you in previous matches: This goal is a very common one. We all have players we struggle with. But sometimes just getting over this hump can accelerate a player quickly up to a higher level. First, this may require achieving more basic goals for improved strokes or changing to different tactics and strategy.

These are just a few of the goals typically set by tennis players. You will, no doubt, have some others as well. Try to take them one at a time. Be patient with yourself. "Rome wasn't built in a day."

ACHIEVING GOALS – Can be very rewarding – to juniors as well as parents.

If you are one of those "world champion dreamers," more power to you. Keep your distant goal in mind as you set goals building up to it. Be determined. Make the commitments necessary. Do your tennis homework. Pay your dues. Believe in your self. Enjoy the trip. The journey may be more rewarding than the destination. But the destinations can be very rewarding as well.

Our whole family will never forget our daughter Karin's eighteenth birthday dinner at home. We were all seated and ready to have our meal when the phone rang. I answered it and it was Gail Godwin, the women's tennis coach at UCLA. I called Karin to the phone. Gail announced to Karin that she had a full tennis scholarship for her to play at UCLA. What a birthday present! Karin had always wanted to go there so her dream was fulfilled. The rest of the family was thrilled, as you can imagine. Especially thrilled were Gretchen and myself. Gail did not realize that it was Karin's birthday which made the surprise extra special. Karin's achievement was very rewarding to her and to her mom and dad.

This was, indeed, a dream come true and the fulfillment of many goals set by Karin prior to that night. We had all worked as team. I was coach. Gretchen was the ever-vigilant mom who provided inspiration and transportation. Her brothers, Jim and John, were practice partners as well as her severest critics. These were bonding experiences for all of us as we experienced them. We all benefited in many ways.

I've related this story to demonstrate the fullness of what can happen when goals are set. Some are achieved. Some are not. But the knowledge that dreams are the inspiration that spark goals to be set is very rewarding in itself. You're not always going to reach that distant dream but each goal achieved gets you closer to it. And the road along gives life

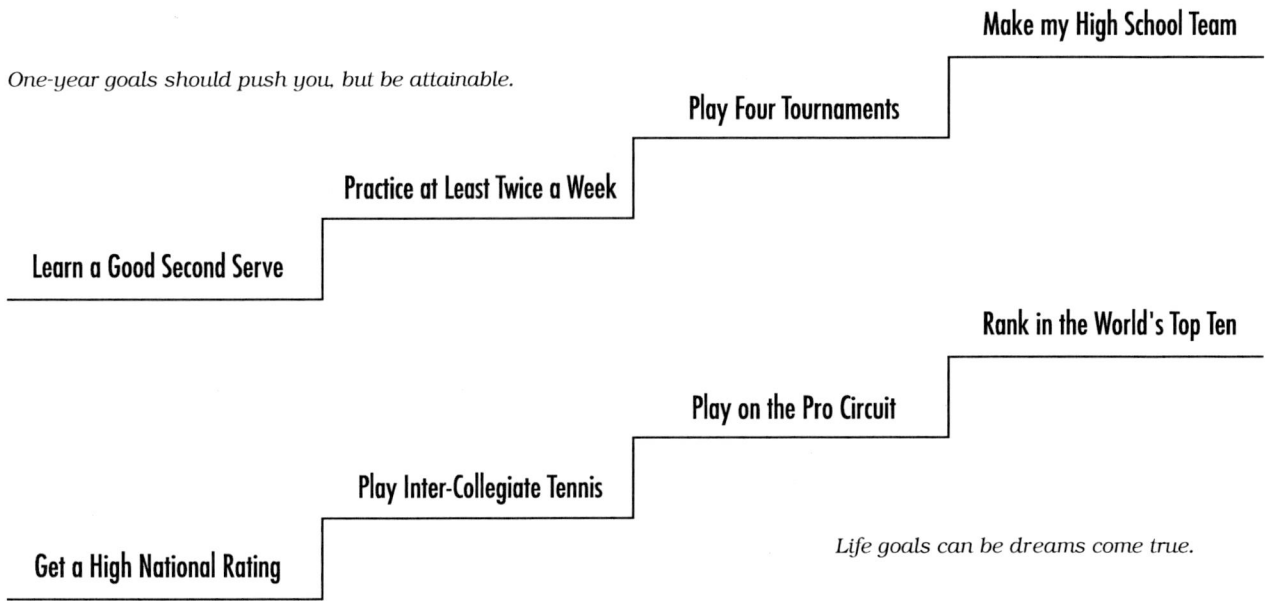

One-year goals should push you, but be attainable.

Make my High School Team

Play Four Tournaments

Practice at Least Twice a Week

Learn a Good Second Serve

Rank in the World's Top Ten

Play on the Pro Circuit

Play Inter-Collegiate Tennis

Life goals can be dreams come true.

Get a High National Rating

experiences that can be as rewarding as achieving the goals themselves.

The goals achieved don't have to be scholarships to college or winning major championships. Parents and kids are rewarded when even the smallest goals are achieved. I've had young children doing a drill where they must bounce the ball ten times with their racket. When they achieve this you would wonder if there were any more joy in Heaven than on the faces of both the parents and these kids.

So my advice here is to encourage the dreams, make the goals attainable and enjoy the road to each goal. The rewards will take care of themselves.

Loren Thaxter doing her "bounce down" practice.

Andrew Penman doing his "bounce up" practice.

LEARN TO PLAY DOUBLES – It's your IRA

Can you ever imagine getting old and still playing tennis? Well, for you kids reading this, if you stay healthy you can play tennis as long as you want to. You'll even be playing pretty well when you are an old 30 or 35. In fact, you might play some very good tennis even later than that. The USTA has national championships for 90 year-olds.

As you grow in age and in the game what will you play most often, singles or doubles? If you're not sure, take a look at what's being played regularly at your local courts. And check out all those older players who are excited about their NTRP league team. I'm pretty sure you're going to see a lot of doubles being played.

What's my point here? Well my point is, that later in life, you'll probably be playing plenty of doubles, even if you still like singles. Doubles is, of course, a very different game from singles. Different shots and strategies are required to play the game well. You need to learn a good kick serve, quick volley technique, when and how to lob, how to hit overheads and most of all, how to return serves effectively.

For lots of kids these strokes and techniques don't seem very important now because singles is about all they play. Only a few junior tournaments offer doubles events. This is sad. The doubles game compliments singles play. John McInroe was a better singles player because he played doubles as often as possible.

It's also sad that doubles is not as highly regarded as singles by touring professionals and their fans. The money and glamour are in singles for both men and women. This fact influences young players to focus primarily on singles, I'm sure.

Don't overlook opportunities to play doubles as a young player. You will benefit from doubles play and it will be a game for you to enjoy greatly later in life.

Playing with older players can be very

(Left to right) Jeff Wolpert, Steve Lempel, Steve Blumberg, and Bill Rogers love to play their clay court doubles matches.

(Left to right) Loren Thaxter, Alana Early, Grant Stanley, and Steven Johnson learning to enjoy some doubles.

enlightening. Rather than blasting hard shots as you might in singles, doubles play requires more finesse. When you're older you won't have the strength of youth but you won't need it in order to play good doubles. This is one of the reasons older folks enjoy their doubles.

So why have I said you should learn to play doubles, it will be your IRA? IRA stands for Income Retirement Account. It's a financial account people put money into while they are working so they will have savings to use when they retire. Putting some effort in now to learn doubles will assure you of tennis enjoyment later when you don't want to or can't play singles anymore.

So get your buddies out there to play doubles with you. If you become a good doubles player it could make the difference in being chosen for your school team or possibly winning that important last match for your team. While you're enjoying doing this, you'll also be building up your tennis IRA.

Come to think about it, you could even call it your TRA, Tennis Retirement Account. Learn to play doubles while you're young. You'll be glad you did.

WHENING TENNIS – You can't do any better.

A "homonym," according to Webster, is a word with the same pronunciation as another that has different meaning. Winning and "Whening" are sort of pseudo homonyms because I've really made up "Whening." It's not a word found in Webster's Dictionary. I've also twisted the true meaning of homonym because I want my readers to understand that you truly win when you apply all that I'm talking about in this book on *WHENING* TENNIS. So in a way, these two words mean the same thing and therefore cannot be homonyms.

Success is another word important to this discussion. Webster defines success as a result or outcome and amplifies this by saying that success is a favorable or satisfactory outcome or result. I think it's safe to say that everyone likes success. We like favorable results in the things we've undertaken. Winning a tennis match is a favorable result for one player and an unfavorable one for the other. There are no ties in tennis.

The philosophy of *WHENING* TENNIS is that success doesn't always include one's having the highest score. Please notice here that I haven't said that winning cannot be part of *WHENING* TENNIS. It certainly can be.

It is even possible to win with the highest score and not succeed at *WHENING* TENNIS. This happens occasionally in a tennis match. I've seen players taunt and patronize their opponent and still win the match easily. Yes, and I've also seen players cheat horribly to win a match. There is a constant battle with coaches who illegally signal players during play to help them win their match. Players who allow these things to happen during their matches have made winning the only thing. What a pity. They could be reaping so much more from their playing experience. Moreover, losses often become devastating. When winning is all there is the pressure on players, parents, and coaches can cause great and damaging fallout for all involved.

Pride is another operative word I want to add to this discussion. It can be a word describing exaggerated self-esteem or conceit. I like another of Webster's definitions which defines pride as delight or satisfaction in one's achievements. This is the kind of pride I'm talking about in *WHENING* TENNIS.

When success and pride are viewed in their proper perspectives and when all the factors of playing with maximum physical and mental effort are combined then *WHENING* TENNIS has been accomplished. You've played the game in the best possible way. You can move on secure in the knowledge that you did your best regardless of the score.

The importance of a *WHENING* TENNIS philosophy will be carried over into life's experiences. This is one of the main reasons I have felt inspired to share it with my readers. Tennis brings out one's personality. Your personality is shaped dramatically during tennis matches. When your opponent hits a winning shot that barely touches the line and it's match point, you must call the ball "good" no matter how much it hurts. This is real character building. There are very few other sports that require this degree of honesty and responsibility of a player.

When you have built your game and goals around a *WHENING* TENNIS philosophy you will be able to make the line call described above and still be able to move forward. Disappointed no doubt. That's normal and all right. But your success and pride will remain in tact because you've played all your matches with a *WHENING* TENNIS state of mind.

LOSING TENNIS – Shake it off – but learn something.

No one wins every match. The best players in the game lose many matches on the way up. Most of them will tell you that they learned more from their losses than they did from their wins.

I had an interesting losing experience my freshman year of tennis at UCLA. In those days athletes had to play freshman sports for one year before they were eligible for varsity play. I was in a tough match that I tried very hard to win. Unfortunately, I lost 7-5 in the third set. As I walked off the court, my coach JD Morgan walked toward me. I hoped he would give me some words of encouragement and helpful advice. Instead, he looked me square in the eye and said, "Huebner, you played just well enough to lose." Well, I hardly knew what to say. JD was a hard man to please but had a winner's attitude for sure. He later became Athletic Director at UCLA and did a fabulous job. I learned that day to shake off my loss and that I'd better get the last point of any matches I'd play for UCLA.

You are going to lose plenty of matches as well in your tennis life. The question is how can losses help you? Have you analyzed them? Do you want to learn from them? If you answered these latter two questions in the affirmative then you've also answered the first one. Losses magnify our weaknesses. Sometimes those weaknesses are mental, sometimes they involve tactics and strategy and sometimes are just plain poor stroke fundamentals. You need to be open to all possibilities. You need to make realistic, honest appraisals of losses.

- Did you go into the match with overconfidence? Remember the John Wooden advice to "never think you are better than your opponent but always think you are just as good."

- Did you play your opponent's weakness too much until that tactic really hurt you? This actually happens on occasion. Did you change your tactics and strategy too late to avoid defeat? Or were you winning the match and then changed to another game plan which caused you to lose?

- Did you allow a distraction to spoil your concentration? This can happen when bad line calls are made, either by opponents or lines persons. It can also happen when opponents create distractions. You have to learn not to let these things bother you.

- John Wooden instilled another gem in his players: "Failing to prepare is preparing to fail." Perhaps, in retrospect, this is why you lost your last match.

I cannot, of course, enumerate all the causes for loss here. Suffice it to say, you are the one who knows best why you lost. But perhaps you are not the best judge of the reasons. Coaches "earn their keep" by helping players with this. Even buddies who watched your match can sometimes be very helpful. You don't have to agree with these other opinions but you should always be grateful for them. Others have good intentions and are usually trying to be helpful.

Disappointment is part of losing. It's okay. Discouragement sometimes follows as well. I've burned my rackets in my imagination more than once after losses. But you have to shake off discouragement as well as disappointment and move ahead. The next match is right around the corner.

Getting too disappointed and/or discouraged during a match is a no-no. Great players shake off service breaks and losses of important games or sets with more determination for what lies ahead. Once a point is finished it's history. The same is true for service breaks and losses of sets. But as long as there is "light at the end of the tunnel," you must stay positive.

There is value in analyzing wins as well as losses. All losses should be examined and tough wins are valuable to analyze as well. If you can make some losses be of help you will have made the most of them.

My final admonition to parents and/or coaches is to let the losing player live with their feelings for a while before starting a critique of the match. Emotion can cloud reason. A little time given before discussing the match usually makes for much better dialog between coach and player.

Mel Taylor, an aspiring junior player at the Fig Garden Swim and Racquet Club in Fresno, California, writes notes after important matches.

PHASE SEVEN
CHAMPIONSHIP REQUIREMENTS

CONCENTRATION – Focus on what you're doing is number one.

Where is your mind when you play a match? Does it want to wander? Do you struggle with extraneous thoughts? Are you too tired to really care? Is your mind saying, "Lets just get this thing over with and get off the court?" You're an unusual player if, at least occasionally, your answer is not "all of the above." I think it's safe to say that everyone has these thoughts from time to time during matches. So you are among friends if you did answer "all of the above". The trick is to be able to mentally "snuff" these thoughts so you can get back to the task at hand. That's what the champs do. And often, at every level of play, it's the player who can keep concentrating who wins.

How do players maintain their concentration? What can you do to overcome these distractions that spoil your focus on what you want to do?

Here are some hints that have helped me the most:

- Slow down. You can do this between points. You don't want to slow down so much that it becomes a stalling tactic but you don't have to hurry. Take your time. Use your speed during the point.

- Bring your thoughts to the present. Thinking about what just happened in the previous point or what might happen three games ahead doesn't help at all. Zero in to the "now."

- Get your mind on your side of the net. You can't be thinking about what your opponent is wearing, doing, or saying. You can't really control those things but you can control what you're doing.

- Go back to fundamentals. You need to do this if you're missing shots you normally make.

- Work harder. We all get a little lazy once in a while. Moving your feet, preparing earlier and staying aggressive will put your mind back in the game as well as your body.

- Keep your emotions under control. Concentration can be lost during emotional outbursts. Sometimes it takes several points to recover your focus. In the meantime crucial points can be lost.

- Play the point in progress. Your concentration has to be aware of the score but you can only play one point at a time. Concentrate on the point at hand and what you have to do to win it.

- Condition yourself. When all things are equal the player who is in the best physical condition will be able to maintain their concentration the longest.

You want to be as consistent as possible during match play. Ups and downs in concentration make for inconsistency and inconsistency produces big point losses and service breaks.

When fans see competitors on the Futures and Challenger circuits play they often wonder why these players aren't playing at a higher level. They hit the ball with all the flair of the top players in the world. What's the difference? The difference is that these players have not developed the intense concentration required to fully maintain point, match, and tournament consistency.

Lack of concentration and positive thinking leads to lower self-confidence and tentative play. Experience is the great teacher that can help players overcome these tendencies.

I remember the first time I traveled away from my hometown to play a tournament. I was awed by the new surroundings and had difficulty concentrating while playing. Later, when I played intercollegiate tennis out of state and at world famous places like Forest Hills in New York, I knew I had to put extraneous thoughts out of my head if I wanted to do my best on the court. The second time I played out of town, out of state, or at a prestigious tennis facility it was much easier. These experiences add maturity to every player.

Focused concentration leading to self-confidence and positive play manifests itself at every level of play. Players with lower seedings, rankings and NTRP ratings have to concentrate on not being intimidated when playing higher level players. When match point arrives for you to upset a higher ranked player your concentration will be severely tested to be sure.

At lower levels of play a lack of fundamentals often makes the difference between players. However, players who don't have the physical game can make up for this lack with better concentration. If you concentrate and play more consistently you'll be surprised by what you can accomplish. As the old saying goes, "Tennis is definitely a thinking person's game."

BE REALISTIC – Playing within yourself.

I had an old friend Edward Kaldunian, whom I knew when I played most of my tennis at the Roeding Park courts in Fresno, California. "Eddie" said "that every tennis player thinks he can beat every other tennis player." I think he had a handle on what a lot of players think about their game. I don't think Eddie was deceived about what he could do against a world class player. But like the players he was referring to, I really think he felt he could at least win a game or two from almost anyone.

Players like to fantasize about how well they can play. Their benchmark for every shot is based on the best one they've ever made. The idea that that shot has happened only once in a lifetime isn't part of the consideration. The thought is that if I had to I could make that shot again. Good luck.

Now these examples are somewhat exaggerated, I'll admit. But not being realistic about oneself can often lead to disaster in shot selection, not to mention in winning matches. If you're a 3.5 NTRP rated player, on the average you're not going to make shots like a 4.5 NTRP rated player. What's more important is that you shouldn't be trying to. You have to realistically assess where you are in tennis ability. Play the percentages. Sure, occasionally, you need to *go for it.* But overdoing this will put you so far behind in errors that it will be impossible to catch up with spectacular winners.

The other unrealistic failure is always wanting to play better players. It's true that playing up lifts a player's game. It isn't true, however, that playing with contemporaries or lesser players will ruin your game.

When I was a tennis director, I had one woman refuse to play on a 3.0 team. She was rated a 2.5, really felt she should be a 3.0 and insisted that she should be playing on a 3.5 team. I knew she would lose miserably if she did but this is an example of how some players are totally unrealistic about their games.

In most shot selection situations you know what you can do and what you can't do. Players who learn to play "within themselves," who are not trying shots that are beyond their ability in given situations, will have a great deal more success. "Overplaying" shots is the term often used to describe this kind of error. Don't flatter your opponent by trying to make it so good. You don't have to. Challenge your opponent with shots that stay in the court. You'll be ahead of the game more times than not by being realistic.

DIFFERENT GAMES REQUIRE DIFFERENT MENTALITY –
Serve and volleyers versus baseliners.

Clay court players really hate to play on grass. Conversely, grass court and even some hard court players do not do their best on clay. When you've played most of your life on a particular surface you develop certain instincts and strokes which work best on that surface. You're comfortable playing on your home courts.

It's amazing how the court surface dictates almost everything. Your grips, the way you stroke forehands and backhands, the way you serve, and even what you do with your volleys can be totally different from one surface to another.

Moreover, without even realizing it, players develop a mental set for their play. You just can't be successful going against the style the court surface demands. Also, while you're learning to play on a given surface you don't develop strokes and shots which are ineffective on that surface. It's perfectly natural that strokes and shots develop that work the best in game situations. Whether you want to or not your mentality is shaped, as well as your physical game.

The two opposite mindsets, for fast courts like grass and slow courts like clay, are basically creative and reactive. There is a certain amount of both of these focuses in the repertoire of all top players. But for players who want to serve and volley and who chip and come to the net as soon as possible every point, the primary thinking has to be creative. In contrast, the primary thinking for slower court players is to react to what their opponent does. Many clay court players are content to just wait for opponents to miss or impatiently come to the net so they can be passed. These two opposite ways of playing become instilled in players to the degree that trying to change from one focus to the other is very difficult. It's not just the lack of the physical strokes that players struggle with. Mindset and instincts, I think, are even more difficult to change when playing on a foreign surface.

I first noticed these differences when I played tennis for UCLA. All of our conference matches were played on hard courts. When we competed in the National Intercollegiate tournaments we played on clay. We had to make considerable changes in our play to compete. The NCAA powers-that-be wouldn't dare require this today.

One of the other problems is the difficulty many intercollegiate players have playing doubles. So many of the young players come up as back court specialists. They have played a reactive style all their lives. You can't play doubles with that mental set.

As I mentioned earlier, clay court players have a distinct distaste for grass court tournaments. They just can't bring themselves to come in behind their serves. And when they do they often are not confident in the volley position. The same goes for big servers who like to end points quickly. They get impatient and are not used to the longer backcourt rallies required on slow clay.

Two interesting examples that go against what I'm saying here are what Bjorn Borg and Pancho Gonzalez did during their careers. Borg was one of the greatest clay court players of all time, yet he won on Wimbledon's grass five times. He was able to do it because of his great athletic ability. He lifted his game and did serve and volley but he was so quick afoot that he was still able to defend on grass. Gonzalez had the big California serve and volley game. Yet he was patient from the backcourt and was able to come in and be very successful on clay. My old friend Tony Trabert, who was a wonderful serve and volley player, also had great success on clay. He won the French Open on clay as well as Forest Hills when it was played on grass. These players and the great Rod Laver were able to adjust their mental games and make the most out of their physical attributes as well.

It's not easy to do this. I guess that's why the grand slam of tennis is so difficult to achieve. Competition among the world's best players is so tough today that winning the four Grand Slam tournaments on all surfaces is almost impossible.

One other point is that hard court players, as a rule, learn to play aggressively. When they get the chance they will come to the net but they mostly try to volley with depth rather than short. This tactic is modified instinctively on clay with shorter volleys and drop volleys.

I also want to point out that this creative versus reactive mentality develops not only because of the way the ball plays coming off the various court surfaces but also because of the different footing on each surface. Hard court players have good, sticky footing on cement and asphalt. That's not true on the natural grass and clay courts. The fact that the footing is more slippery on these surfaces influences the strategy and tactics and therefore the mental set for play.

These different surfaces are what add the spice and variety to tennis. I think it makes the game exciting. If everything was played on only one surface I guess you would have a better benchmark for rankings and seedings. However, the challenge and history of each of the surfaces have made the game attractive to people all over the world. Also winning on the different surfaces is what makes the Grand Slam so elusive.

The challenge for all of us is to learn to be creative and be reactive when necessary. Learning to be an all courts player will broaden your perspective of tennis and add to your ability to play wherever lines are drawn and a net is up and ready for play.

BE PATIENT – But stay aggressive.

When you make your move can be just as important in winning a point as what and how you do it. Impatience can really kill you.

Before I get into the patience and aggressive dialog for playing points, I have to tell you a little story about my wife Gretchen's patience/aggressive move one day at the courts at Sub Base in Pearl Harbor, Hawaii. At the time I was an Ensign serving aboard the destroyer USS Walker, so we were living in Pearl Harbor government housing, not far from the submarine base. We had gone over to the courts at Sub Base to play a little tennis. When we got there two fellows were playing, so we sat down to wait until they finished playing. We waited patiently for twenty minutes or so but the men didn't appear to be finishing. I took a bathroom break and when I returned Gretchen was out on the court talking to the older man. She had decided to be a little aggressive to see when they might be finished. I was astonished that she did this because I recognized the older man. He was Vice Admiral Stumpf, Commander in Chief of the Pacific Fleet. I thought I was a goner and might be reduced to a regular seaman if he took offense. Gretchen came back to where we were sitting and said that the man was extremely courteous and said they would be finished shortly. Was I relieved! Gretchen was, in this case, patient and a little aggressive and thankfully it worked out just fine. But now let's get into what you need to do when you're playing tennis.

You need to balance your patience with an aggressive mental set. Patience alone won't cut it in a lot of point situations. Just being patient with nothing more won't help you take advantage when you should. Balancing patience with aggression is an art. It takes some players a long time to develop this balance. Some never learn and it can be a mental stumbling block that keeps players from advancing to higher levels.

The first step in playing points is to learn patience. Beginning and intermediate players are handicapped to a degree by fundamental flaws in stroke production. Physically, they simply cannot keep the ball in play. Players at these levels may have the patience but their lack of solid stroke production holds them back. This is another strong argument for working hard to develop sound stroke technique. If you find yourself in this predicament you know what you have to do: practice, practice, practice is the answer.

When you can extend the points comfortably without making easy unforced errors you'll be ready to add some aggressive shots to complete the balance talked about above.

It always amazes me how many tennis players would rather win a point with a winning shot than win one through an opponent's error. I guess that's human nature but both results count the same in the score. This propensity results in downfall in so many instances. And the desire to make this winning shot results in players playing points without enough patience. When anxiety takes over during a point it usually results in an error or an opportunity for the opponent to make a placement winner him/her self.

The art of playing the game that I spoke of in my introduction is exactly what is important here. All the factors need to be in your computer when you are trying to be patient and aggressive. You have to consider not only your own capabilities but your opponent's as well.

When your patient and aggressive strategy is to develop a point, but stay in the back-court, you must weigh your opponent's ability to defend from his/her back-court. When you are working the point to eventually come to the net you have to weigh how well your opponent makes passing shots and/or lobs. And which side, forehand or backhand, do you want to come in on? Do you want to hit up the line, crosscourt, short, deep, up the middle, hard, higher and slower, with topspin, or underspin? Wow, does all this have to be digested to play patiently and aggressively? You bet it does.

You're going to find that by playing patiently you won't always need to finalize your strategy with a winning coming in shot or put away volley. Your opponent will often miss before you have to finish. The side benefit, you might call it, is that by being patient you didn't have to make a winner to win the point. The patience part of the equation did it for you.

Percentage tennis is such an important concept. No matter how good a player you become this concept will always be important in your play. You want to raise your percentage for success during play for each point. You'll be doing this by working points until the time is ripe to make your aggressive move. And when you make this move it shouldn't be made recklessly but with high percentage in mind.

This particular section illustrates one of the obvious facets of *WHENING* TENNIS. When you make the right choices during a point and win the point, you have combined the "when" with the win. A satisfying combination to be sure.

DEPTH IS IMPORTANT – For keeping control.

Angles are important for shot placement in tennis. Most of the time players are very aware of the ones that go from side to side. The forgotten angles are the up and down ones. The up and down angles, combined with speed and spin, are the ones that dictate depth. And the depth of many of your shots will determine your control of the point in play. Let's take a look at some of the instances where depth makes the difference.

- Depth of your groundstrokes – Playing your forehands and backhands deeply into your opponent's court keeps him/her in a more defensive posture. Giving an opponent a short ball often ends up with a placement you can't reach. Conversely, when your shots are hit deeply into your opponent's court you will often have a short return that you can put away.

- Depth on lobs – Short lobs will be a delight for your opponent. But keeping lobs deep drives your opponent away from the net and makes it much harder to make a point winning overhead. Good, deep lobs can neutralize your opponent's net advantage. Playing deep lobs can also keep your opponent on his/her heels so your passing shots are easier to make.

- Depth on drop shots – This shot is used only occasionally but when you use it you better make its depth short and just over the net or you'll give your opponent an easy winner. Slower, softer court surfaces make it easier to be successful with drop shots.

- Depth on passing shots – These shots often need shorter depth to be effective. Rolling, dipping passes are very difficult to volley. In this case shorter depth is what you want. However, sometimes you need longer depth because you are so far out of court that your pass needs to carry to reach the inbound portion of the court.

- Depth on serve – This is particularly important on second serves. You simply can't allow your opponent an easy short one to return. You will find yourself in trouble immediately if your serve goes too short.

- Depth on return of serve – Controlling this shot's depth depends on the situation. When you're playing singles and your opponent is not coming in behind serve you want your return to go deeply into your opponent's court. When your opponent is coming in behind serve a shorter, dipping shot makes it harder to volley. A low return forces the volley up so you can often get a good chance to pass on the next shot. When you are playing doubles your opponent will be coming in behind serve almost always. So, you want to hit your return low to make your opponent volley up. When you return low to the incoming server's feet your partner can often poach and make a put away volley. Learning to use these different depths for the appropriate situation will put you in a good controlled position.

- Depth on volleys – In first volley situations, when you've come in behind serve or a groundstroke, your shot depth is very important. When playing on hard courts deeper is usually best. When playing on clay or grass a short volley can be more effective than a deep one. When playing doubles you want your volley to go down at your opponent's feet so he/she has to volley up. Playing the right depth in each situation will make it more difficult for your opponent. The depth is every bit as important as the direction.

- When you are on the receiving end of shots with varying depth you need to react as soon as possible. Your opponent's shot depth is harder to read than side to side direction. When you move early for these different depths, whether it's deep on your baseline or a drop shot, you'll be able to make your best play. You'll be controlling the depth on your side of the court. When you control the depth of your shots you'll be controlling your opponent on both sides of the court.

SERVE WITH A PITCHER'S MENTALITY – Keep 'em guessing.

Don't you love it when your opponent serves to virtually the same spot and with the same speed every time? I do. It gives me a chance to groove my return. And, even if I've had some trouble with my return, it gives me a repetitive chance to make corrections.

Players who don't vary their serves are very often on the wrong end of a service break. Even hard serves that are consistently placed the same way become easy to return when the returner gets used to the pace.

On the other hand, when servers vary the speed and spot into the service court, the returner cannot be so well prepared. I'll use baseball as my example here. If pitchers don't vary their pitches they can get bombed by the batter. The changes compliment each other. A change up after a fastball is more effective.

And so it is with serves in tennis. Almost everyone has a favorite spot to serve to. However, like baseball, if players insist on playing that serve too often they will have their serve broken more often than they would like. The exception, of course, is when you discover a weakness in your opponent's return. Then serving to that same spot frequently makes perfect sense.

Learning to hit to different spots in the service court takes some practice. You need to get your basket of balls out and find an empty court. If you really want to improve your service this is what it takes. You'll find that there are little things you need to do to place the ball differently. It will probably take you out of your comfort zone to do this. When you've done the same thing with your serve for a long time your whole service feeling is grooved to do just that.

The down side to serving with this "pitcher's mentality" is that you might get clobbered on some of the changes you make. But the long run picture will be a positive one, I'm sure. You'll get used to thinking "spots" when you serve and with repetition and practice you will automatically do the right things to make your serve hit that "spot."

An important part of this is not to telegraph to your opponent what serve you're going to hit. It should be possible for you to hit all your different serves with the same grip and service motion. You might need to vary your toss a little but it's hard for your opponent to read this if you don't change too much. The main difference should be where your shot hits the service court, not how you do it.

If you're not already playing your serves with a "pitcher's mentality" I advise you to begin thinking this way. You will be adding a new dimension to your game if you do.

RETURNING SERVE – More important now than serving?

All points in tennis have to start with the serve and return of serve. Gaining advantage immediately depends on which player makes the best one of these two shots.

I used to watch Pancho Gonzalez practice with Don Budge at the Los Angeles Tennis Club. Budge had a great return game and Gonzalez was a great server. It was a classic match up to be sure. Those were the days of wooden rackets. Another one of the same classic match ups has been Pete Sampras and Andre Agassi. Their graphite weapons have added even more firepower to their exchanges. In these battles it always seemed that whoever was "on" that day would dominate.

It does seem that as time goes on and rackets become more powerful and courts are slower, the serve has been somewhat neutralized. The emphasis has shifted from the serve and volley to serve and aggressive backcourt play.

Returning serve for winners and to gain initial advantage is especially evident in women's tennis. Only a few of the women have really big serves but almost all of them have good returns. Women who have to serve a lot of second serves find themselves in trouble a good deal of the time.

As a rule the men serve more aces but they get clobbered as well when they have to make too many second serves.

When you look at the way the game has changed, at the top level especially, the trend seems to favor players who return well over top servers. Why has this happened?

First of all you have to look at the space each shot must be placed. Serves have to hit into the service court. A returner knows this and can prepare. Returning second serves is a little like having a high bouncing short ball during a backcourt rally. Moreover, the returner has the whole court to hit to. Consequently, the server cannot prepare as easily. The returner has the advantage of using this larger space to either pass the opponent coming in or drive the opponent out of court even more than the server can.

Secondly, today's rackets are much quicker because of the materials and methods used to manufacture them. When a ball is struck with a graphite composite frame it comes off much quicker than it did with wooden rackets. This quickness translates into shots that penetrate into the court sooner, which makes them hard to anticipate and return.

A third but more subtle thing is the fact that, as a match progresses, it becomes easier for a returner to read where the serves are going. Also, as the match progresses and fatigue sets in, unless the server is really strong, the serves lose a little of the early match "pop" they had. This might not make a lot of difference at lower level play but it can give the returner a slight advantage toward the end of a match at the top level.

The old saying that "a good offense will beat a good defense" is probably true. When the server can maintain his/her highest level throughout a match it is very difficult for a returner to get a service break. The server's offensive clout is too tough for the defensive returner.

Maintaining this level isn't easy. Just a small lapse in concentration or a couple of great returns can break the match open. This is when the returner goes on the offense and the server becomes defensive. Then the return has become as important as the serve.

It certainly is in doubles. Serves cannot be hit at a returner's feet. And no one gets his or her first serve in all the time. Good returns in doubles keep poachers honest and make servers volley up. It's true that returns are not always down at the incoming server's feet. If they are not they will probably result in an easy volley winner for the serving team. When returns are well placed servers begin to press to make better serves. This can result in more second serve opportunities and more errors from the server.

Another subtle fact that my son Jim brought out is that you only serve once every four times in doubles but you get to return half the time. So you have twice as many opportunities with service return as you do serves in doubles.

The message here is pretty clear. Even if you do not have a natural propensity for serving, and a lot of players don't, you can develop your service return as a real weapon. At least half the time in every match you'll be able to use it.

ANTI-SHOTS – Lifting your game to counterattack.

"All right, that's enough of that." I've said this to myself on several occasions when my opponent was beating me with a certain shot. You've probably experienced this feeling in a match yourself. How can you find an answer? Changing strategy to stay away from your opponent's strength could be one way. However, changing strategy sometimes puts you in the position of playing away from your own strengths. What else could you do?

You might try kicking your game up a notch with an anti-shot of your own. You need to counter your opponent's great shot by doing something better yourself. Sometimes it may require changing your strategy as well as lifting a certain shot. Here are a few examples of anti-shots and strategies:

- SERVE – Your opponent is killing you with great returns of serve. To counter this your first move is to get more first serves in the court. You might have to go with your favorite spot at first to get this consistency. As soon as you feel comfortable you'll want to pick up the pace and move your serve around to different placements. In singles or doubles you may even want to move along the baseline to different service positions. Giving your opponent different looks, placements and speeds are the keys to countering the returns with your anti-shot, the serve.

- SERVICE RETURN – This time your opponent is drilling in big serves. You're struggling with them. Your first step is to shorten up your backswing. Just determine to block the serves back using the speed of the serve. You could also move a little farther back. And you can pressure the server by making him/her pay on the second serve. Lefties give a different look and different spin on their serves. When the spin hits your racket it wants to make your shot go farther right. Adjust your aim to the left to counter this spin. Your goal, as with any anti-shot, is to cut into your opponent's confidence. I've found that exhaling in order to relax as my opponent tosses the ball helps me move more quickly to make the return. Remembering to do this often lifts my service return to a higher level.

- FOREHANDS AND BACKHANDS – It's a tough call when your opponent is pounding you from the backcourt. On given days a player may just be zoning with forehands and/or backhands that are too consistent and not even returnable. Don't give up when this happens. There are many ways to combat this. The object you want to accomplish with your anti shots in this case is to take your opponent out of rhythm. You can do this by changing the pace. Sometimes semi high lobs will do the trick. Or, you can take your groundstrokes earlier. You can slice backhands to keep the bounce lower. You can come to the net more, challenging your opponent to make passing shots. In this case your anti-shots are your semi lobs, coming-in shots, volleys and overheads. Your serve can be an anti-shot in this case as well. Most ground strokers don't like to be hurried. You may get passed if you begin to serve and volley but you'll be rushing your opponent with a different rhythm which may get him/her out of sync. Your choice of which of these anti-shots and anti strategies to use will largely depend on the speed of the court you're playing.

  An interesting example of the application of an anti-shot is the way Steffi Graff used her sliced backhand. Many arm-chair quarterbacks argued that she would have been a better player with a topspin backhand. Steffi knew that topspin makes balls bounce higher and are therefore easier for opponents to hit with authority. She wisely, I think, played this shot to perfection as an anti-shot against the great two-handed backhands of her opponents. During a point she waited patiently with this shot until she received a forehand. Then her opponent was in trouble.

- VOLLEYS – In this case you have been coming in frequently and playing volleys but with little success. You seem to be making coming in shots reasonably well but not winning points you think you should. When this happens it may be because your opponent is making difficult passing shots, which are hard to volley. Or it may be that you are giving your opponent too much time so he/she can hold you with too many options to get the ball by you. When this happens you need to lift your volley to a higher level. You need to control the depth better and/or "stick" the volley with more authority. Remember that when your are in a volley position you are vulnerable to counter attack. You can't afford to give your opponent too much time or that will translate into too many options for the pass or lob. Play your volley as an anti-shot to this defense.

- OVERHEADS – You're coming in often or maybe you're playing doubles so you have to station yourself at net. At any rate your opponent is really lobbing well. Now you have to lift your overhead game to meet the challenge. Whether you are in a singles or doubles game you might want to station yourself farther back, away from the net. You don't want to let the lobs get behind you. Making good judgements as whether or not to let a lob bounce is important. High, defensive lobs are much easier to hit after they bounce. Are you lifting your overhead backswing directly over your shoulder? Are you keeping your eyes on the moment of impact? Is your opposite hand pointing at the ball? These are all basic to hitting good overheads to counter a lob. If you make enough good overhead placements your opponent will undoubtedly stop lobbing. In the opposite situation you must do the same.

- DROP SHOTS – Senior players use this shot much to the dismay of their opponents. A drop volley is another form of drop shot and can be very effective, especially on grass and clay courts. They work the best when they have a little backspin on them. You can't hit them too high or too deep or you know what will happen. If your opponent is making good drop shots against you, you might have to play in closer so you can get to them easier. Keeping your groundstrokes deeper will prevent your opponent from using them effectively. And drop shots are never hit with topspin, so when opponents show a slice stroke be alert to move forward.

Anti-shots require a little boldness. You have to think there is something you can do better. As stated, it may take a different strategy or it may mean just hitting a better countering shot. Whatever you do should be intended to take your opponent out of the winning game that is beating you. Make him/her say "uncle" with your "anti-shot."

PLAN "B" – It could be more important than plan "A".

Jack Kramer was famous for playing his game plan no matter what his opponent did. He was so confident in his serve and volley game that he would continue using it until the match was over. He didn't win every one. No one does. But in the years when he played the hard courts were faster, there weren't as many good clay court players and grass was the playing surface of the major tennis events. Very few players of his day were capable of countering his powerful game. He felt he didn't need plan "B."

Not many players today have that luxury. The best players in the world need an initial plan to start a match. Then they will have one or two others to implement if necessary. You and I are no different. We need to be able to change things when the match is not going as planned. If you have given a match some thought, whether it's singles or doubles, you will play more confidently with a purpose and some backup flexibility.

When you are involved in a match that begins to slip away you need to make a change if you hope to turn it around. That change can be either to alter what you are doing to your opponent or to make an attempt to alter what your opponent is doing to you. These changes often go hand in hand.

Some of these changes are covered in this phase titled "Anti-Shots." Anti-shots are all concerned with lifting your shots to higher levels or changing where and what you're doing to counter your opponent's shots. Here are a few plan "B" changes that are of a slightly different nature:

- Take your time – You may have a pretty good plan but if you are rushing each point you may not be giving yourself enough time to be successful. This changes the rhythm between points. And it gives you some time to think about what you are going to do on the next point.

- Be patient – Trying to make something happen too soon during a point often results in overplaying shots. Be willing to work up to your plan each point even if it takes a long rally.

- Cut down on your risk – Maybe you don't have to make it so good. Giving your opponent a chance to miss may be the best thing you do.

- Be bolder – Show your opponent that you're not afraid to take some chances. Don't panic if you lose a few points doing this. What you want is to take your opponent out of the routine you've been doing.

- Don't get caught doing just enough each point to lose – You may be setting yourself up, time and again, by not coming in on a serve or approach that's good enough. This just gives your opponent the counter punch opportunity that many players thrive on.

- Don't change the angle of the backcourt rallies too soon - Keep the crosscourt play going. Only change to a new direction (down the line) when you have a shorter ball or you have your opponent way out of court.

- When your opponent floats the ball – He/she is trying to buy some time during a point. You need to be on your toes and move in to volley the floater. Whether you swing at the volley or punch it you will often finish the point with a winner. If you've not been doing this it can dramatically change the tenor of the match.

- Change your offensive game to a defensive one – Or you could do the opposite. Many players who thrive on counter punching can't hurt you from the backcourt. So don't let them maximize their game by playing into their hands.

- Play your opponent's strength – Sometimes you have to do this to open up your opponent's weakness. At the same time it's possible that you can crack your opponent by this challenge to his/her strength. The great Bill Tilden was famous for this tactic. He was so confident of his ability that he reveled in breaking his opponent down in this way.

- Staying back in doubles – This plan "B" for doubles is often very productive. Rather that receiving serve with your partner at the net, have him/her play back with you. This formation often nullifies a team that poaches often. It also works to advantage when your opponents aren't volleying well. On a slower court like clay where it's harder to put overheads away a good lobbing team can turn a match around with this change of original plans.

- Changing doubles formations – When your opponents are crushing you with service returns it's sometimes a good ploy to go into an "Aussie" formation. During service games the net person plays in the middle of the court instead of in the service box in front of the receiver. It doesn't always work but it does make the returner think about where to hit the return. He/she can't just think "cross court" on every return.

- Doubles signaling – If you and your partner are not communicating your intentions during service games, hand signals might be a good plan "B." Signaling helps both players know what the other is going to do and can result in some really positive results.

There are many more plan "B's" that you can go to, of course. These are just some of the possibilities. The fact is that if you change from your original plan "A" to something else and you win the match, you've obviously done the right thing. You can be proud of yourself. Plan "B" has become more important than plan "A."

PLAYING THE BIG POINTS – How important are they?

We would all agree that match point is the biggest of the big points and that it's the most important point of any match. Most of the time it's the toughest to win because when anyone is down match point he/she or the other team is going to go all out or the match will be over.

The world's best players are, generally, aware of all the important points in a match. They realize the situation. These players will be doing their utmost to win these points in order to keep control or to regain control if that is what is required.

My old friend Whitney Reed, who was the number one player in the United States in 1961, always played tough on match points for and against him. However, Whitney always played to the crowd and couldn't resist a chance to clown a bit. On one occasion, before he became number one, he and his partner Hugh Stewart, had Art Larsen and Herb Flam down match point in the doubles final of a big tournament in Palm Springs, California. At the time Art was the number one player in the country and Herb was top five at least, so it was going to be a real upset for Whitney and Hugh if they could just win the last big point. I was among the crowd watching the final. (I had lost in the singles in a good match to Tony Trabert.) Another old friend George Druliner, was umpire for the match. With Whitney serving and Hugh at the net, a serve whizzed over Hugh's shoulder for an ace. He thought the match was over so he reached out to shake hands with Art and Herb. The whole crowd broke out in laughter, as did George in the umpire's chair. Whitney had thrown up two balls, hit one of them and served his ace. When things quieted down they played the point over. I honestly can't remember who won the match. The big point to win the match was so humorous I don't think any one remembers the outcome as much as the "ace" served by Whitney on match point. This kind of incident could only happen when tennis was still an amateur sport. However, the big point importance was what made the incident so humorous.

All big points are so important that winning or losing most matches hinges on them. It's quite possible to be in a match where you're just hanging on because you are winning these big points at important times and your opponent or opponents are not. I've been in matches where I really felt I was losing most of the points but I was coming out ahead in the score because my opponent or opponents just weren't winning the big points. I've been in the opposite situation as well.

Second to match points in importance are service break points. Holding serve has always been tantamount in tennis. So when break points occur for the receiver or receiving team, an extra effort is required on both sides of the net.

Thirdly, points leading up to a service break point are obviously also important. When the score is thirty all both players or teams want the next point.

There are other situations that make some points more important. For example, if you are right handed and you're playing a lefty who is putting you in the bleachers with serves in the add court, winning points on the even court becomes more important.

I've always felt that the first point of a game is important. When you get this one, whether you are serving or receiving, it's a boost to confidence as well as putting your opponent in the hole right to start. Baseball pitchers like to get the first strike for the same reason.

Another instance when winning a point is important is when you're in a really long rally or you and your opponent have made some incredible gets to prolong the point. Psychologically, it becomes a small victory for the winner of this kind of point. Sometimes it turns a match around.

What can you do in these big point situations to increase your chances of winning them? Throughout my competitive years, I've found that doing the following things have helped me:

- Get your first serve into play. You shouldn't wimp it in but you shouldn't be overly aggressive either. A little more spin or a little less speed can often make for a better first serve percentage. Think of it this way. When you're playing as the returner wouldn't you like to see a second serve on a big point? So get your first serve in, especially on game, set, or match points. Don't give your opponent/ opponents the luxury of hitting your second serve on these points.

- Get your return into play. Don't give your opponent a free point off his/her serve. "Make 'em play it" is one of my favorite expressions.

- Be aggressive. Don't try "silly bugger" shots on big points. Lobbing is the wrong shot to use unless your opponent has a terrible overhead. You've got to make a good service return or go for the pass if your opponent comes in. A drop shot is also a "no-no" unless it's pretty obvious that your opponent can't reach it.

- Use your best shot. I think this is a good play most of the time. If you serve well down the "T" in the add court, even if your opponent has a good right hand forehand, I would go with that placement, for example.

- Play your opponent's weakness. This is the best call on many occasions. You would do this especially when you're coming to net behind a serve or groundstroke. You don't want to give your opponent a chance to "not think" by counter punching in this situation with their best shot.

There are probably as many options as there are point situations when playing big points. These are just a few hints that I hope will help you in your decisions to play them. Sometimes the hardest thing is just to keep your concentration. You must stay calm and take your time on these points. Being in too much of a hurry to get the big point over with can be your downfall. It's also very important not to let losing a big point "get to" you. You have to put each finished point behind you and move ahead. There will always be more big points to play in the future.

PERFECT BOTH BACKHANDS – One isn't enough anymore.

There have been major changes in the game as I mentioned earlier. There have been some subtle changes as well. When top players develop different strokes and ways of playing there have to be reasons for these changes. The pendulum swings the way it will.

Pancho Segura from Ecuador and Jack Bromwich from Australia were players of the past who used two hands rather than one. This was considered quite unusual in those days. Most of the other world class players in their era played one hand for both their forehand and backhand shots. The interesting question is why has the two-hand backhand become more prominent in the modern game?

Analyzing this as a player gives me some clues. First off, as a one hand backhand player myself, my biggest weakness on my backhand side is when I have to hit a high bouncing ball. I can chip it but that's essentially a defensive shot. I can't get over the high bounce. Therefore, I cannot punish the ball the way I wish I could. Consequently, I must chip a high bouncing serve to my backhand and the same with a high bouncing groundstroke. Two hand backhand players don't have this problem. They can really smack a high bouncer on service return or groundie. I mentioned before that the hard court surfaces have become slower which makes balls bounce higher. I also mentioned earlier that modern rackets have caused players to use a lot of topspin that also makes for high bounces. So this is where a lot of shots need to be hit. Voila, a couple of the subtle reasons for using the two hander.

I think another reason for the shift to the two handers has to do with the speed of play today. The shots are just flying off the high-energy rackets being used. This results in many groundstroke shots having to be played on the rise. Players do not have time to back up to let the ball come over the bounce for a comfortably timed shot. And, tactically, players cannot afford to be pushed too far behind the baseline for fear of giving potential groundstroke angles to an opponent. Taking the ball on the rise requires exquisite timing. These shots are easier to make on the forehand side with one hand. However, hitting a half volley, as it were, with a one-hand backhand is another story. When players have two hands on their backhand there is more security to hit this shot. Then it's almost like playing a forehand. This must be a better way to hit these shots or so many players would not be doing it.

The speed of play has also encouraged players to hit backhands with an open stance so they can recover to center more quickly. I think using an open stance has a downside in that it makes it harder to hit down the line, a very important shot. Top players should learn to hit down the line with as much confidence as hitting crosscourt. Lots of repetitive practice will perfect this key shot.

The other side of the coin is that top players must also perfect the one hand backhand as well. The chip shot is still needed when you have to stretch for wide backhands. It is also needed for short, low chip coming in shots.

And not the least of the reasons for developing a one hander on your backhand is to get more comfortable on the volley. So many lower level players who have two-hand backhands struggle with the backhand volley. They are used to the support of the other hand and cannot trust their primary hand to make good volleys. The backhand chip and backhand volley go hand in hand. When you can make one the other is relatively easy. To do this you have to get comfortable without support from your other hand.

Playing your backhand with only one stroke doesn't cut it if you want to elevate your game to a high level. It's not enough to hit everything with two hands or everything with one hand. Determine to perfect both and you will be able to deal with anything your opponent throws at you. It's a different game than it used to be.

ANTICIPATION AND FOOT SPEED – What they add to your game.

Quickness about the court adds immeasurably to your playing arsenal. Or if your opponent has this ability, it can mean trouble for you.

Maureen Connolly dominated women's tennis in her era. She had the nickname "Little Mo." She got this moniker because she played shortly after World War II, in which the battleship Missouri played a prominent role. "Little Mo's" groundstrokes were compared to the mighty guns on that battleship. She also had great foot speed and good anticipation that served her as well as her powerful groundstrokes. She could get to almost everything her opponents would hit to her.

Ichiya Kumagae from Japan, who became my good friend, played with great foot speed and anticipation against players of the Tilden era. Later Ken Rosewall and Vic Seixas used their great speed and athleticism. On the distaff side, Steffi Graf ran down most everything and probably could have been a track star. Other players, such as Michael Chang, Martina Hingis, and Lleyton Hewitt, have also used their foot speed and anticipation to harass opponents.

Every era has had its speedy players. Virtually all had some weakness but most made up for this with their quick movement about the court. This ability to move with such speed helped them become far better players. Why did this help them so much?

The answer is that their speed put extra pressure on their opponents. This pressure caused their opponents to press or overplay at times, which created errors and sometimes even loss of confidence. This one asset is often more productive than any particular stroke. One other advantage of good foot speed and anticipation is that having them enables players to get to shots earlier. This means that these players will be "playing the ball" and "not letting the ball play you," as described in Phase Four. When this happens a player has the ball under better control and has a chance to play different shots. He/she has options. When you're just barely reaching a shot you don't have time for much more than just getting the ball back.

Also, "early" is often better than "hard." By that I mean when you get to the ball earlier you can hit to the open court before your opponent can recover. When you wait too long you'll need to make a more difficult shot and probably have to hit it harder. How many times have you been at the net only to let a soft shot drop too low so you had to volley up? If you had closed to volley earlier when the ball was higher and safer to play and before your opponent could recover, you probably would have made an easy winner.

Foot speed and good anticipation work equally well for both genders. Girls and boys, as well as senior players with these gifts have a definite advantage over slower opponents. You can add the ability to anticipate to your game. If you also have foot speed this combination can add immeasurably to your success in matches. To gain better anticipation at any level of play you simply need to train yourself to respond more quickly to your opponent's shots. When I teach beginners I often explain how much more time they will have if they react immediately as the ball leaves their opponent's racket. Expert players do this. Intermediate players don't start to move until the ball passes the net. And beginners don't begin to move until the ball bounces on their side of the court.

Certain anticipatory skills come with maturity in the game. When you see a right-hand opponent toss the ball for serve well to his/her right you can bet he/she is going to serve a slice, probably to a right-hand receiver's forehand. When you see your opponent slice a groundstroke you know it's going to bounce lower. When a certain pattern develops time and again in your opponent's game you begin to anticipate this and can be waiting for it. There are other clues that help you anticipate. You get better and better reading them as you grow in the game.

When beginning and intermediate players watch the world's best players they can hardly believe that anyone could be ready for such hard shots. They begin to realize that they too can be ready, when they respond as early as the pros do.

If you don't have natural foot speed you can improve with a regimen of jump rope workouts. That is, if you want to make the most out of the speed you have. Sprints and other speed work can be of value also.

By adding these two, foot speed and anticipation to your game, you will be adding another "stroke" to your repertoire. This addition will serve you well as it has those world championship players mentioned above.

EMOTION ON THE COURT – Help or hindrance?

John McEnroe's on court emotions have been an overwhelming force in his identity as a tennis player. His "out of control" behavior has become a source of continuing debate among tennis fans. He is rarely ever mentioned in the press without some remarks about this provocative trait. Did this help or hinder his match success?

Pancho Gonzalez, Art Larsen, and, way back when, even the great Bill Tilden showed their emotions at times when they played. How about these players? Did they benefit from outbursts at ball boys and girls, linespersons, or referees?

On the other hand, the remarkably unflappable Bjorn Borg and the business like Maureen Connolly showed virtually no emotion as they played. Most of the tennis players over the years have just played, keeping their emotions to themselves.

Some players damage their own games when they emote using body language. I remember watching the great Ken Rosewall who, on occasion, would drop his head and mope around the court when he was losing. I have been guilty of poor body language at times myself. I can assure you that it didn't help either Kenny or me. It won't help you either.

The answer as to whether expressing or holding the emotions in, as helps or hindrances, is undoubtedly individual in nature. We are talking here, of course, about what demonstration or non-demonstration of emotions does to add or detract from the player's performance during play.

Coaches need to know the emotional makeup of each player they work with. Some players need to let off steam to play better. Some can direct inner anger into stronger physical play.

The important thing, I think, is for coaches and players to understand the boundaries of gamesmanship and sportsmanship that demonstrations of emotions must maintain. When these boundaries are crossed, whether it helps the player or not it damages the play, the game and in fact, the player him/her self. At this point, in my opinion, the demonstration of emotions has gone too far. Winning at any cost has gone beyond the philosophy of *WHENING TENNIS*.

I'm sure these demonstrations are what outrage the public tennis fan. Demonstrations can enhance the excitement but can also detract from the beauty of the game. Too much is too much. I think I speak for a lot of tennis fans when I say that I'm embarrassed when emotional outbursts are overdone in a match. I love the game, the mounting pressures, the great shots at crucial points and I don't like to see this beauty overwhelmed by emotionally out-of-control scenes.

I hope I haven't disappointed you by not finalizing whether emotions can help or hinder a player. As I've said, it's an individual thing. The bottom line is that emotions should not go "out of bounds," impacting play. Players need to respect the game, the officials, their opponents, as well as themselves when they are on the court. The help or hindrance question applies to the game as well as the player.

THE BIG PICTURE – How far sighted are you?

Gaining championship status as a player includes many bumps in the road. The steps up the ladder are not always up. Unsuccessful matches and goals not met seem to impede progress. You have to lose a few battles to win the war.

Being disappointed when these losses occur is perfectly natural. The disappointment can be quickly erased when you remind your self of the long term. You must have a "big picture" in mind to be able to do this. Keeping the big picture in mind involves everything from the match you are playing to the ultimate goal you have in tennis. Let me explain further.

A match is part of the big picture, the goal of the moment. To be a championship player at any level you cannot let any downturns interfere with achieving this goal. I've seen top level players let one little thing bother them so much that it causes them to lose a match. Perhaps this kind of player doesn't make each match a part of the big picture.

Another big picture example would be where you want to be in the rankings at the end of the season or year. You may have some losses you don't think you should have but you'll be able to put them behind if you keep the big picture of the season or year in mind. This will enable you to look forward to the next match with a positive attitude.

You might look at the final big picture as if it were a graph, something like tracking a common stock or business progress. You're going to see some downturns but ideally the general trend should be headed up toward your ultimate goal.

I think having a big picture in mind, or you might call it an ultimate goal, will help you assess your progress and decide whether or not you are being realistic. Everyone doesn't make it to the top. When you see how you are doing as the matches and years go by, you may have to adjust your big picture. If you have imagined the big picture, done everything you could to reach it and realistically see that it's more than you can do, it's not demeaning to make a change. Your calling may be in some other arena.

There is a satisfaction itself in "making the effort to do the best you are capable of doing," as John Wooden has put it so succinctly. If you have done that I think you would agree you've given your "big picture" your best shot. Surely, the travel has enhanced your life despite not reaching your biggest picture.

CONDITIONING – Be ready to go the distance.

In all sports finishing is more important than starting. Teams and players, who start strongly but run out of gas, are often disappointed with their results. Physical fitness is part of playing virtually every sport. Tennis is no exception. Being in shape to play is the base that every player needs to be able to go the distance as well as prevent injuries.

When players are younger they naturally have a high energy level and flexible bodies that can withstand the rigors of playing tennis. Quick movements and stamina are required, however, for players of all ages. And I don't mean to imply that top level juniors don't need physical training. They do.

I think it's especially important for middle aged players to stay in condition. Players at this age, it seems, are susceptible to straining muscles and what have you. They still have the strength of youth but they struggle to prioritize time for physical conditioning. Muscles and tendons need to be used to be flexible enough to prevent injury.

The pre match warm-up is a very important discipline. Most World-Class sports figures do this but so many recreational players do not. You should make this a part of every match you play regardless of your ability. When you finish your match you should also take some time to stretch and warm down. I'll bet you're agreeing with me as you read this. I'll also bet that you're not doing it.

Strength training has become more important in all sports. Basketball players used to be wiry, now most of them look like wide receivers on a football team. Strength is important for tennis players as well. Being able to control difficult shots, move quickly, and pound hard shots throughout a match requires lots of muscle. Tennis shots are mainly propelled with good timing but strength helps too.

One of the strongest players I ever encountered was Lew Hoad from Australia. Even though Ken Rosewall was called "muscles," it was his buddy Hoad who was extremely strong. One day, on the grass court circuit at the South Orange Lawn Tennis Club in New Jersey, we were all in swimming after the matches. The Aussies began to play "horse." This game requires one person to sit on the shoulders of another and people try to topple each other over in the pool. At one point Hoad put both Ken MacGregor and Ken Rosewall on his shoulders. I was amazed that he could move around in the water with two people perched above him. He wasn't very tall, I would guess about 5'9", but very powerfully built. His tennis was very powerful as well.

Gene Mako, a grand slam winner, was an incredibly fit person who played before tie-breakers were invented. He and Don Budge were two of the top players of that era. Gene developed shoulder problems and had to shift his tennis tactics from serve and volley to, in his words, an "I can't miss a ball" strategy. Keep in mind that sets had to be won by a margin of two games and that some sets went up to forty games and sometimes more to conclusion. In spite of this Gene played singles, doubles and mixed doubles in every tournament he could. In today's game virtually no one does this. In fact, many players today only play singles but still complain about fatigue from having to play five sets every other day. To the modern player's credit, it's true that there are many more tough matches than there were in Gene's day. This fact and the energy that must be expended playing consecutive tough opponents, are the reasons that players today don't enter multiple events.

Aerobic training pays off when matches go three or five sets. Matches can last for four hours and more. When temperatures rise long matches naturally become more draining. As matches drag on in these conditions the body begins to weaken and so does the mind. What happens then is that the player who is in the best condition can continue to concentrate. When a player loses concentration he/she is finished. Besides anaerobic conditioning for strength and prevention of injuries, I think aerobic conditioning is the most important physical fitness. Like foot speed and anticipation, conditioning is like another "stroke" in a player's arsenal. These "extras" in a player's game can be the difference for players who compete at club levels as well as players at the top.

Some players have natural stamina even if they don't train. Art Larsen, who played a long time ago, was this type of player. He won a lot of matches in five sets but his conditioning regimen left a lot to be desired. Instead of drinking water he often consumed a six pack of Coca-Cola during a match and he seldom went to bed before 2 am in the morning. And he smoked cigarettes constantly. Everyone who knew him marveled at how he could sustain play in a long match.

One time, when we were all playing one of the grass court circuit tournaments at South Hampton, Long Island, Art had made it to the semifinal. He was to play Frank Sedgman the next day, so several of us urged Art to get a good night's rest. He reluctantly agreed to go to bed at 10 o'clock. He couldn't play a lick the next day and Sedgman defeated him in straight sets. Apparently, the extra sleep made him very lethargic. I'd never seen him play so poorly. Frank was favored to beat him but I think the break in Art's normal lifestyle really did him in. It goes without saying that I don't recommend Art's type of training program.

But if you play tennis once a week and work out a couple of times a week, you'll at least be on a minimum program for your own championship tennis. The pros who make tennis their business, must of course do much more. They cannot leave any stone unturned if they want to be in the hunt in the highly competitive professional circuit. At all levels of play the better-conditioned athlete is usually the one who gets the toys at the end of long matches.

CONFIDENCE – Earn it and you can keep it.

Championship players must have confidence in themselves throughout a match, throughout a tournament, and throughout their career. But confidence is such a fleeting thing. It comes and goes for athletes in all sports.

There are three levels of confidence. One can be under confident, confident, or overconfident. To reach championship levels in tennis players must find the middle ground here. Disaster lurks on either side of genuine confidence.

There are numerous answers to what it takes to have confidence. Some people are supremely confident of everything they do. I think it's good to be inherently confident but one must be realistic as well. When tennis players are not realistically confident it can translate into overconfidence. This can be devastatingly harmful on the tennis court.

I think real confidence is obtained when you earn it "the old fashioned way." Tennis players have to go through this earning process for each stroke, the use of the strokes, the strategy of play and all the other skills involved. When a weakness is known there is low confidence in whatever it is. Real confidence can only be obtained by overcoming the weakness, by earning the right to be confident about it. When you can do what you could not do before you will know it. You can feel the confidence. It's real. This is the kind of confidence championship tennis players must have. This confidence produces winners when needed. When this happens in a match mental dominance follows.

Tennis is such a mental game. At the top levels of tennis most players can hit virtually every shot. When all other things are equal it's often the confident mentality that makes the difference between winning and losing.

Also, confidence goes up after a good win or playing in a prestigious tournament and goes down after losses. I've always liked Kipling's "If" in which he says, "If you can meet with triumph and disaster and treat those two imposters just the same...." One who has real confidence is able to deal with these two imposters and move ahead to the next match.

I've had my opportunities to deal with these imposters. One incidence still makes me chuckle when I think about it. I was playing in the National 40 singles at the Monticedo Country Club in Santa Barbara, California. I was seeded but lost in the first round. My confidence was pretty low at the tournament dinner that night. My old friend Hugh Stewart was asked to whistle to entertain all of us. Hugh could whistle incredibly well. After his entertaining presentation he asked if he could say a few words. The crowd of about one hundred people, knowing Hugh's bright wit, encouraged him. He said he just wanted to console Larry Huebner. He said Larry had been a triple loser in the tournament. First, as a seeded player, he lost in the first round. Second, he was staying at the Motel Six, and thirdly he was now on his way back to Fresno. The crowd loved it. And I couldn't help laughing either. He actually helped me forget my loss, regain my confidence, and deal with the imposter that seemed so disastrous.

In my next match I remembered to follow Coach John Wooden's advice from his father. His dad told him, "Never believe you are better than your opponent but always think that you're just as good." Coach passed this on to many athletes at UCLA and inspired us to have a balanced confidence when we were competing.

When I got back to my beloved Fresno I went to work on some of the weaknesses I felt had caused the loss. My confidence returned as I sorted out these problems and I got my game back on track. I urge you to restore your confidence in the same way when the need arises.

PHASE EIGHT
CURRENT TOPICS OF CONVERSATION

TENNIS IS A GREAT CARRY OVER SPORT –
Schools should emphasize it in physical education curriculums.

I know I need to exercise. If you are like me pushing weights or doing laps bores me to death. Thank God I have my tennis. Playing has always given me great pleasure plus the exercise necessary for good health. I was lucky. My dad got me on the court at a very young age. It still seems that all children need their parents, friends, or someone to introduce them to the game.

All our schools should be introducing students to carry over sports by offering required classes in tennis, racketball, squash, golf, or swimming. These are all physical activities that can be taken into later life. This, I think, would balance academic education carry over with physical education carry over.

Whether they realize it or not our school administrators are making couch potatoes out of far too many students. Sure it's great to play team sports like football, basketball, and baseball but how many kids who play these sports in school continue to play them after graduation? Not all students are going to like tennis. I'm aware of that. But being exposed to carry over sports in a required curriculum would establish a base for future playing possibilities. I've met so many athletes who wished they had learned tennis even though they were stars in the major sports. Very few make a living from sports they played in school. Too many former athletes live vicariously later in life as pro sports fans sitting on their couch or favorite chair with a beer in one hand and some junk food in the other. These former school athletes may be doing wonderful things at work with their academic education but their physical education has really let them down.

This can't be what educators want I'm sure. The biggest problem is that educators are stymied because of the cost to install the proper facilities in their schools. The public rejects bonds all too often, even for the basic academic needs. How can we, in America, get out of this dilemma?

I think it might be possible to utilize facilities already operating in many cities across the country. In the last twenty or thirty years, tennis, swim, and racquetball clubs have sprung up everywhere. Virtually all the clubs have professionals who run the club programs. And almost every middle school and high school has buses. Students could be transported to nearby clubs for classes two or three times a week to participate in professionally designed classes in these vital carry-over sports. Clubs and pros would have to meet certain standards, of course. And there would be costs to these programs to use the club pros, the bussing, insurance, etc. However, the costs should be considerably less than installing the facilities on the school grounds.

There would be clubs and professionals that couldn't qualify and some that would choose not to participate. However, I think quite a few clubs would welcome the additional, steady income. The clubs would derive a certain amount of public appreciation for their involvement. And there would be exposure as well for their club for future or even present day family memberships.

Since I have been involved in club management myself I know that there are slow times during the day when hour-long classes could be offered with minimum impact on member use. Classes could be offered during winter months when member use is lighter. This would be attractive to most pros because of lighter lesson demand at this time of year. It would be up to the school districts across the nation to initiate these programs. Districts with clubs meeting the proper criteria would have to join forces to make such a program happen.

A more excellent way to do this, of course, would be for school districts to provide enough tennis courts at schools to run a program on campus.

A wonderful example for school districts to follow is the district in Clovis, California. Years ago when a friend Dr. Floyd Buchanan, showed me some plans for a tennis facility at Clovis High School, I was overjoyed. He was the Clovis District Superintendent at the time and I had been teaching his daughters to play tennis at the Fig Garden Swim and Racket Club in the neighboring city of Fresno.

Many years have passed since then and many courts have been installed at the schools in the Clovis School District. Dr. Buchanan made sure when each new school was constructed that a large battery of well-designed tennis courts were included in the plans. He also made school courts available to the public during off school hours. Consequently, Clovis now has a booming tennis community. I'm quite sure that many of those students who took tennis classes in Clovis schools are now enjoying the public play that these courts provide.

When Dr. Buchanan made the decision to include tennis facilities for all the Clovis schools he did a wonderful thing for the community and the people in it. Kudos to Dr. Buchanan. More districts should follow his example.

My hope is that school districts will take action to create more emphasis on teaching carry over sports, especially tennis. If they do a better balance will be struck between academics and the physical exercise everyone needs for a lifetime of better health.

LEAGUE VERSUS TOURNAMENT PLAY – Which one's for you?

Winning national championships is not just for the most talented players in the country anymore. The United States Tennis Association has introduced thousands of players of all abilities across the country to a league format. These National Tennis Rating Programs (NTRP leagues they're called) make it possible to use handicaps so players can compete with their contemporaries. Players at all levels of competency can be national champions, which is a totally new concept. National tournament play is still popular but many players have opted for playing on a team in the leagues.

There are a number of differences between league and tournament competitions. For adults these differences have shifted more players away from local tournaments and into sectional leagues.

I think one of the main reasons for this shift is the shorter commitment of time for league play. Time is so precious these days. When you enter a tournament you have to commit to a full weekend or two or even several consecutive days. League play usually takes place during an evening or on a weekend morning or afternoon. The total match is often finished in two or three hours. Team practice is arranged, as well, to suit the player's time frames.

There is pressure in team play but it is not as intense as the individual play in tournaments. You can lose your individual match in team competition and the team can still win. In a tournament, if you lose, you're out whether it's singles or doubles. You might get to play again if consolation rounds are offered but being out of the main draw is the end of any championship hopes.

The comradeship and sense of value shared with the team is a different feeling from the individual emphasis of tournament players. Team members really get excited and cheer for each other. This is fun for everyone on the team but this seldom happens among tournament competitors. It's "all for yourself" in tournament formats.

Junior players are the ones still playing the tournaments. There is no nationally organized league for them to play. There is sectional play called "Team Tennis" for novice boys and girls but nothing leading up to a national championship. The main reason juniors play the tournaments is to get sectional and national rankings. These rankings can lead to college scholarships and positions on sectional and national teams. Juniors selected for these teams get special coaching and invitations to major tournaments. And, it goes without saying that these scholarships are worth big money. League play for juniors could be a good idea.

I think that USTA league play has attracted a lot of new players into a competitive format that is brand new to them. Many have never played in sports competition. And for various reasons, some adult tournament players have also shifted into the leagues.

Playing in leagues doesn't mean that you can't also play in tournaments. Lots of players do both. The advent of USTA leagues has just added more playing opportunity for everyone. Most of all it's made competitive play reachable for lower level players as well as more expert ones.

You never know, a gold ball for a national championship in USTA league or tournament play may be just around the corner.

TENNIS ELBOW – Have you ever had it? I hope not.

I know. It hurts when you hit your backhand, or your forehand, or maybe it hurts when you hit your serve. It even hurts to pick up a salt shaker. I hope I'm not talking about you but if I am, I think there may be number of things you can do about it.

Before I get into remedies I'd like to point out why I think people get this damnable malady. When you look around the courts where you usually play you probably see a number of players using some kind of elbow brace or support. You may be using one yourself. But think about all the world's best players that you have watched. How many of them have you seen wearing an elbow device? I can't recall any one, as I think about it. Why is this? They are hitting the ball many times harder and more often than you do. This has got to tell us something. I think it gives us some clues about how recreational players can prevent elbow problems. It also gives us clues about why proper fundamentals are worth their weight in gold.

The pros work out consistently doing preventative maintenance on forearm muscles and tendons. You can do this too, by just squeezing an old tennis ball in your hand a few times a week. Being fit is a very important part of the game.

As for the fundamentals I want to take you back to Phase Two, where I talked about smoother swinging with a little more mass in your racket. And also to Phase Three, where hitting the ball out in front and holding a good ready position are important. Then to Phase Four, where not applying these fundamentals can be so unhealthful.

The best players in the world have to be pretty fundamentally sound or they wouldn't be playing at that level. This tells us that minimizing strain on your body, by using all the leverages possible, will help prevent unwanted discomfort. For my game and for all the teaching I've done over the years, "hitting the ball out in front" is the prime fundamental. Everything follows this one: grips, weight transfer, follow through and good contact. This fundamental is, therefore, the pacesetter for all strokes.

There are ways to minimize and eliminate tennis elbow. In Phase Two, I mentioned lowering string tension. Here are some other possibilities:

- Before you play soak a towel in warm water and wrap it around your elbow.
  Leave it on for three or four minutes to get the area warmed up.

- After you play apply some ice to the area. Keep plastic bags in your racket bag so you can do this immediately after play. Most clubs and courts will have a source for ice.

- If you have pain in your elbow try using one of the elbow devices offered for sale at most tennis pro shops. They really do help.

- Ask your doctor if you should take any pain medicine before you play. Drugs of this kind usually help reduce inflammation as well as pain.

* Make sure you are using proper grips for your strokes. Gripping the racket improperly may be causing you to hit the ball late. You might need some professional assistance for this.

- Do you really know where you want to contact the ball? If not, ask your pro to help you with this too. When you get sideways for most of your shots and you meet the ball the right distance out in front, your troubles should begin to disappear.

- Try wrapping your racket handle with an over grip to make it a little bigger. This will sometimes help to keep you from squeezing your grip too hard.

- Speaking of grips, you shouldn't be holding too tightly between shots. Keep a soft grip during your ready position. Holding your racket tightly all the time is wrong anyway and could be causing the extra strain.

- A medical analysis might be the right road to take. Your physician can help you with this.

- The last piece of advice I'm going to impart is to just lay off tennis for awhile. This is hard to do when you love to play the game. But because tennis elbow is basically an inflammation, this may be your only cure. You may have to pay this price to get back to the courts when you feel better.

Dealing with tennis elbow has always been somewhat of an enigma. I've tried, here, to help you know the causes and possible cures. I truly believe the strains come mostly from hitting the ball too late.

I count myself lucky to have never had tennis elbow. I hope you've never had it either. If you have I hope one or more of the suggestions I've made will keep you playing the game of a lifetime.

SPORTSMANSHIP – Has it died and gone to Heaven?

One of the great sportsmen in tennis history was a German player named Baron Gottfried von Cramm. He played during the great amateur tennis days before World War II.

Don Budge, in his book A TENNIS MEMOIR, tells some stories about Cramm's wonderful sportsmanship. In one instance, at match point against him and his doubles partner in a crucial Davis Cup match, a shot from his opponent nicked Cramm's racket. No one but Cramm noticed it but he called it against himself, even though it meant losing the match.

Don Budge, A Tennis Memoir (New York: Viking Press 1969)

Budge also relates a story in his book where Cramm politely told Don he had been a bad sport in a match he had watched him play. At hearing this Budge says he felt devastated and couldn't imagine what he had done. Cramm had noticed that, when Budge had been passed cleanly by his opponent, the linesman had called the ball out. Budge thought the call was in error and so he responded by dumping his next return into the net in what he thought was a gesture of good sportsmanship. Cram explained that Don, in so doing, had embarrassed the linesman in front of all the spectators and had usurped the right of the linesman to make the call as he saw it. Therefore, it was a selfish display of bad sportsmanship. After the conversation Budge agreed with Cramm and said that he abided by linesman's calls for the rest of his career. Cramm's definition of sportsmanship extended to everyone involved in the match.

I'm sorry but I can't imagine many players today with this depth of sportsmanship. This is not to say that there are no good sports in men's and women's tennis. There are many. Unfortunately, times have changed. Unsportsmanlike conduct is all too often displayed in all segments of the game. All too frequently one sees it in junior tennis, adult league tennis, and intercollegiate tennis as well, not to mention professional tennis.

The worst incident I can recall was as follows: Two players were sent off to play an early round match at a site away from the main courts. They played and when they both came back to the scorer's table to report the score, the loser said she had won 6-4, 6-4. The winner was flabbergasted and insisted that she had won by those scores. Since no official was present when they played the tournament director had no choice but to have them play the match over, this time in the presence of an official, to be sure. Can you imagine the chutzpa for a loser to do this? Little wonder that tournaments today are required to have referees, linespersons, and monitors for matches.

I think many players today have allowed their sportsmanship to succumb to the pressure of money, its prospect, or winning regardless of how it's accomplished. The basic idea of being a "role model" who demonstrates honesty, high standards, fairness, and just plain right and wrong, has taken a back seat to winning at all costs.

Professional players are idolized around the world. Impressionable juniors are especially influenced by their actions. Enough time has passed since tennis became professional in 1968 for some bad impressions to overshadow the good sportsmanship so valued in the amateur days. And, I think it has damaged our game.

Somehow golf has retained its image of good sportsmanship. As for me, I like to watch all sports, especially tennis, for the game being played, the shots made, the pressures that build up, and the high standards of sportsmanship displayed. So I still enjoy watching a golf match. I don't need the dramatics of berating lines-persons and referees, or taunting opponents to make a tennis match interesting. I guess I'm just a "shut up and play" type of guy. I still watch a lot of tennis matches but from time to time the on-court behavior just makes me uncomfortable.

Occasionally, when good sportsmanship is displayed it's a breath of fresh air for everyone watching. It isn't a show of weakness nor is it damaging to one's game. It does, however, add immeasurably to the stature of the player as well as the game.

Sometimes younger players overdo being good sports with their line calls. My wife Gretchen and I had to teach our children to be fair to themselves as well as to their opponents. When our daughter Karin, was starting to play tournaments as a ten year old, she gave her opponents points when balls were out a foot or sometimes more. Lots of kids do this. And I guess if you had to choose, you'd rather have to make this correction than the other way around.

Later, while playing on the WTA tour, Karin was awarded the Karen Kranzke sportsmanship award. It was certainly an honor to be counted among such great players as Evonne Goolagong, Chris Evert and Kim Clijsters who have also won this award.

Sportsmanship will never die, much less go to Heaven. And as long as tennis pros and coaches instill a spirit of sportsmanship in their students the great tradition will be carried on. International, national, sectional and local organizations have all come down pretty hard on abusive conduct of any kind on the court. It's too bad that it has become necessary to set and enforce rules for this important aspect of playing tennis.

Sportsmanship has definitely not died. It's very much alive and a pleasure to see when it's voluntarily demonstrated in a tennis match.

NATIONAL TENNIS RATING PROGRAM – It's not perfect.

Your rating tells everybody how good you are, or how bad, right? Golfers have been playing games with their handicaps since handicaps started. You've got one handicap at cocktail parties and another when betting starts on the first tee. Golf has set the precedence for this waffling way of using the system. Now that the United States Tennis Association has followed suit with the National Tennis Rating Program, tennis players have followed golfers in the same way.

A golf handicap is determined without subjectivity as long as players put their real scores in the computer each time they play a round. If they don't do this it's just garbage in – garbage out. Honest stroke scores for each hole played make a difference as well. So even golf handicaps can be tilted one way or the other and therefore are not necessarily perfect indicators of playing ability. Unfortunately, tennis ratings, handicaps as it were, are even more difficult to administer and assign with accuracy.

Prior to the NTRP system, players in most local tournaments were rated alphabetically as "A" players, "B" players, "C" players, etc. This system at least separated players into categories of similar playing ability. People still had one rating for themselves at cocktail parties and another on the tournament entry form. This was also a pretty fuzzy classification with virtually no objectivity in it. Sandbagging trophy freaks were a problem for tournament directors in those days but the NTRP system has now somewhat cleaned up this problem. USTA sections around the country used to offer rating sessions. Players signed up for these opportunities for "raters" to see them play in order to establish a "visual rating." Self-rating to start is another twist that may be an even better way. When players get on a team and start their league matches the scores are entered into a computer. As the playing season progresses these scores determine whether or not the visual rating was correct. If a player wins too many matches too easily during the season they can be "bumped" to a higher level for the next season of play. Sometimes players are "bumped" down because of their losses. This "bumping" process is somewhat mysterious and often appears to be subjective.

But sometimes players are rated, establish their rating with match play and then at crunch time are given the heave ho in local playoff matches. "Raters" hover over matches at the end of the season and if someone looks too good, "bam," they're disqualified. The team can then lose all the matches a player won, as well as lose the player. There's something wrong here. This kind of subjectivity hovering over teams during the season has made players doubt the system's objectivity.

Ratings are adjusted at the start of the season so teams can be formed. Some players are bound to improve during the season but I still think they should be allowed to finish with their team and the rating they started with.

The USTA has made progress by initiating the NTRP system. There are extensive rules in place and training is given to "raters" who make the initial "visual" ratings. Most of the players rated are at lower levels so raters don't have to be expert players themselves. Even though each level, 2.5, 3.0, etc. have requirements to meet, whether or not they are met is a subjective judgement by the rater. Self rating is a newer option that hasn't solved the problems either.

I don't see how there can ever be a perfect rating system. Moreover, all the rating says is that most of the time the player plays at the designated level. Everyone zones once in awhile and plays at a higher level. And we all have our off days as well.

I do think the NTRP system has shut down the sandbaggers to some extent. If you have a rating you can play "up" but you can't play "down." You're in the computer so you're hooked no matter what you say at cocktail parties. Computers are perfect with what's put into them. People are not perfect, just forgiven.

FUTURE CHAMPIONS – How will they have to play?

Tennis players, like all other sports participants, keep getting better. They are bigger and just as strong and fast or faster than players of past years. Track and field athletes continue to break records, baseball-players hit more home runs, and basketball players perform magically in their sport. But as time goes by the improvements become more difficult and harder to achieve.

In track and field, baseball, and basketball, the equipment hasn't changed much over the years. It's been the athletes who have become more skilled. The equipment used hasn't had much influence on the improvements. Sure some improvements have been made with running shoes, and baseballs and basketballs have been made more uniformly consistent. Since the equipment in these sports hasn't changed much you have to conclude that it's the athletes, themselves, who are setting higher standards in each sport.

But tennis players have had to catch up with the vast improvements in rackets since the wood racket days. The difference in energy released from wood and modern composite graphite rackets is huge. I've mentioned these changes in Phase Two. The new technology has changed the game.

Tennis players have pretty much adjusted to these changes by now and I don't see major changes in equipment happening in the future. A similar status has been reached with track and field, baseball, and basketball, where the athletes are performing at virtually a maximum possible level. Certain athletes will stand out but raising the bar keeps getting more difficult. What will men and women tennis players have to do in the Twenty First Century, and onward, in order to be the best players in the world?

First, let's start with the fact that the court size today seems smaller than it used to be. I don't mean that court dimensions have changed any more than a basketball hoop is placed any lower than it used to be. But like basketball where play is above the rim all the time because of the size and jumping ability of the players, bigger tennis players who also have foot speed can cover court better, thus appearing to make it smaller. More athletically gifted women as well as men have, so to speak, reduced the size of the court.

Second, with the stiff composite rackets the ball leaves the strings with tremendous velocity. Serves have reached the 150-mph level for men and 120-mph level for women. And faster groundstrokes have forced players to use an open stance, even on backhands, so time can be saved to better cover court.

Third, and most important, is that future champions must be able to keep up an intense level of play throughout a match. When an individual or team plays better than their opponent it's the intensity of play the loser cannot match.

When these three factors are considered the importance of certain skills becomes apparent. There are, of course, many things that go into the making of a champion. Too many to list here. But presuming that many world class players have most of these traits, I think the following additional skills and tactics will be required of future men and women tennis champions:

- They must have very reliable, powerful serves. There is no surface - clay, grass, or hard – on which a big serve is not a most valuable asset. Players must be fundamentally sound and confident about their serve. Serves must produce big points when needed.

- They must have a punishing service return. I talked about service returns in Phase Seven. Now it's becoming as important as serving. Great service returns can protect against serve and volley tactics and set up points when an opponent must hit a second serve.

- They must follow up when a ground stroke rally has an opponent in trouble. The ground stroke game has taken over the serve and volley game, except on grass. Too many players today get their opponent clear out of court but don't take advantage by coming in to the net. Lack of confidence in the volley and overhead has caused this lack of aggression. Future champions must overcome this hesitancy and play the whole court aggressively. More doubles play would help players learn these skills.

- The next, and hardest skill, will be the ability to successfully change tactics throughout a match. The complete player of the future must have the tools and skill to play the backcourt offensively and defensively as well as serve and volley. When you think about it two of the Grand Slams are played on hard courts and one other is on grass. Grass is an automatic serve and volley surface. Hardcourts have good traction so quick movement to reach volleys and get back for overheads is quite possible. Therefore, three out of four Grand Slams can be played by coming in aggressively, with proper preparation. Players have always been classified as "backcourters" or "serve and volleyers." They are also classified according to their big weapons. So and so has a big forehand. Or so and so has a huge serve. I think when the day comes that a man or woman is feared for their great volley as well as one of these, the future player may have arrived. Being able to use these skills alternately by staying back or coming to the net is not easy. Surprise is the operative word here. The complete player of the future will have to be able to execute change in tactics at will. Very few players in the history of tennis have had this kind of all court ability. Future champions who can do this will be able to meet any competitive challenge.

Between two players who are equal in all the other factors that make a champion, I believe having these four abilities will provide the quickness and intensity that will make the difference. If players can combine all three skills with the heart and concentration to match the intensity of the physical play they will be tough to beat.

The only other factor that I think will make a difference for future champions is fitness and conditioning. As a match goes into a final set, especially in the fifth set for men's play, conditioning will enable a player to continue to concentrate and play aggressively on serve, return, and coming in when an opportunity presents itself. Clay is the true test for this kind of fitness for both men and women.

I want to turn now to what I feel will make future doubles champions, again for both men and women. Doubles is, of course, a team effort. Doubles teams do the best when there is "chemistry" between the players. Two great singles players do not necessarily make a good doubles team. It's quite a different game from singles. Future championship doubles players will have to have good chemistry as well as the following skills:

- Again, the serve is of paramount importance. Servers must hold their service games. A big first serve helps of course but a strong, deep second serve can protect the server effectively.

- I think the service return in doubles can be more important than the serve. Consistently returning hard first serves puts pressure on the server to make a good volley. Returning second serves down at the server's feet makes the server volley up and gives a partner the best chance to poach. It's "king of the mountain" in doubles. Whoever can hit down is usually going to win the point.

- Quick hands and feet are the requirements for good doubles players. Getting in quickly behind serve makes the first volley easier. Quick hands save a lot of points that otherwise might be lost. Players must use these quick hands and feet to augment good volleys and overheads.

When all things are virtually equal between two doubles teams it's sometimes just a lucky let cord or lucky shot that turns a match around. Teams that can play different tactics can also change the direction of a match. Different formations, signals, and talking together are necessary for good doubles team play. And different tactics can be used to advantage on different court surfaces.

Keeping players from "grooving" on returns and net play is important. I remember when I first played the circuit my partner and I came up against Bill Talbert and Tony Trabert at the Cincinnati Tennis Club. As I followed my serve to the net on one of the early points Bill volleyed softly to me so I had to hit up. Trabert poached and crunched a volley between us for a winner. Shortly afterward another similar situation happened. This time I thought, "I'm not going to let Bill hit a soft one again," so I closed quickly. He looked like he was going to do the same thing as before but as I closed he punched the volley and hit me right in the gut. After that I wasn't sure what he was going to do. Bill was a great doubles player. He was also a wonderful guy. I learned a doubles lesson that day.

I think one of the things lacking in today's professional play is that too many players opt not to play doubles. Learning to be a better doubles player will help players in singles. It can be especially helpful for singles players using the coming in tactic to volley when an opponent is out of position. Doubles teaches aggressive play. It emphasizes net play, both volleys and overheads. Young players in good condition should have no trouble physically playing both events.

To stand out as a future superstar in tennis will not be easy. There are so many good players today in both the men's and women's ranks. To be able to do just a little bit more than one's opponent will require heart, determination, conditioning, playing the right shot at the right time and being able to raise one's game to meet the moment. I'll tip my hat to the person, man or woman, who can "rise above the crowd" in this age of high excellence.

WINNING THE GRAND SLAM – Is it possible any more?

Not many players have won all four Grand Slams in one calendar year. Just winning all four is hard enough but winning all in one year is becoming harder and harder for both men and women. It's not considered a true Grand Slam unless all four are won in the same calendar year.

Is it possible any more? What will it take to accomplish the Grand Slam of tennis? And why has it become an almost impossible task? Let's take these questions one at a time to see what it will take and whether or not it's within the realm of possibility.

The answer to the first question is, of course, that it's possible. The main problem will continue to be the intense competition that the men and women face on the professional tour. The money in professional tennis is "bordering on the obscene," so new players are being added yearly in hopes of cashing in on the pot of gold. As long as sponsors continue to support professional tennis more talent is going to be added to the competitive mix. So, it's always possible that some incredible athletic tennis talent may appear on the scene that can win the coveted Grand Slam.

The answer to the second question is that because these four Grand Slam challenges are played on different surfaces anyone winning all four will have to be able to adjust their game to what each surface demands. Many of the men and women on the tour "have the tools." They can make virtually all the shots required. But because grass, clay, and hard courts play so differently it takes different mentality and intuition as well as different mechanics to successfully play them.

Those who have spent their learning years on a specific surface have the advantage intuitively on that surface. What this means is that sometimes during play shots can't be thought out. They must be played so quickly that intuition is what makes the shot happen. When players have played on one surface long enough this intuition is built into their games. Intuition can make the difference between winning and losing when a player used to a surface is competing with one not used to it.

The great champion Pete Sampras is a perfect example to explain these necessary abilities. He was comfortable when he dictated play with serve and volley, so naturally he was very successful on grass. His mechanics, mentality, and intuition all fit the grass surface where points are won or lost quickly. When he played the clay court events his mechanics, mentality, and intuition did not fit that surface as well or the slower time frame for each point. Consequently, Sampras never won the French Open. In my humble opinion I don't believe winning the French was ever possible for him.

In Phase Seven, section B, I have elaborated on the difference in mentality that it takes to play offensively and defensively. I also discussed how growing up playing on a surface produces the mechanics as well as the instincts that work best for that surface. I don't want to be redundant here but these facts bear directly on the subject of winning Grand Slams.

To sum up then, what it will take to win on all surfaces, my thought is that any player, man or woman, must be able to adjust to all surfaces with mechanics, mentality and intuition. And exhibit all the other attributes that champions must demonstrate in the highest-pressure situations. I think conditioning is the most important of all these ancillary attributes a Grand Slam champion must have. The grind of the tour has to be taken in stride. The very best condition is necessary to prevent injuries and maintain the pace of playing match after match.

How difficult will it be to surmount these challenges in order to win all the Grand Slam events in one year? Are there just too many mountains to climb? I think the answer is that it will be something like winning the lotto. There are so many things that need to fall into place for a player to be a Grand Slam champion. My own opinion is that it will probably be easier for a woman to do it than a man. The men's tour has more depth which translates into more potential for upsets. And women play two out of three sets in all tournaments, including Grand Slams. This means that even though women need wonderful conditioning, they don't have as much emphasis on that phase of the formula for winning. Also, women don't play grass in quite the same way as men. The serve is important but most of the women play in the backcourt almost the same as the other surfaces, so they don't have to change their games as much for grass as the men do. When another Martina Navratilova comes along who can keep up with her contemporaries in backcourt play on the slower surfaces, she'll have the best chance at the Grand Slam for women.

Luck will play a part in accomplishing the Grand Slam. All the factors that must fall into place have a bit of luck attached to them. When the luck of the draw, the luck of injuries to self and competitors, the luck of a crucial line call, and many other lucky breaks occur, a player will have a chance at tennis' Holy Grail.

Whoever accomplishes that feat will, again in my humble opinion, be the greatest player, man or woman, who ever played the game.

COACHING PLAYERS DURING MATCHES – Will it make tennis better?

What would happen if coaching players in Grand Slams, as well as all tournaments, was permitted? Would there have to be an asterisk by these new tournaments? The player's wins wouldn't be the same, in my opinion.

Traditionally, team sports have had coaches and coaching staffs. That's probably why the Davis Cup competition started with coaching. Fed Cup, intercollegiate and high school team players are also coached during play. In this regard, most people accept this in the same way they do football, basketball, and baseball team coaching.

One of the arguments against coaching individual tennis players is that it would favor players that had the money to hire a coach. Coaches cost money. Therefore people that couldn't afford the best coaches or any coach at all would be at a disadvantage.

More importantly, I think adding coaches to the mix would change one of the most important parts of the game. It would take away an element of the game that has challenged players since tennis began. The old saying that "tennis is a thinking persons game" would no longer apply. The coaches would do the thinking with players only trying to execute. The challenge of changing from "plan A" to "plan B" would be up to the coach. The "when" would be taken out of *WHENING* TENNIS.

I'm not unaware that coaching is illegally given to players. Hand signals have been the most common form of signaling changes to players. Making coaching legal would, of course, improve the situation. That's the only upside I can think of for allowing tournament players to be coached during matches.

The downsides, in my humble opinion, would be disastrous. Tennis is basically an athletic game of chess. Modifying or eliminating the challenge of having to figure out one's opponent, or in doubles one's opponents, would take away the uniqueness of the sport of tennis. Having to play an entire match with one's own wits is one of the exciting aspects of the game, for spectators as well as players.

Employing someone to do this during tournament play would take the heart out of the game as far as I'm concerned. I hope it never happens!

LET BALLS ON SERVE – Should they be played over?

Traditionally, when a serve hits the top of the net and the ball drops fairly into the service court, that serve is played over. Let balls occurring after the point is started are not played over. Why the rules were made this way is somewhat a mystery. The question of allowing all let balls to be played has been debated for a long time.

A few years ago intercollegiate coaches decided to try playing lets on serve for their men's tennis team matches. Most of the players have adjusted to this new rule and have learned to play on when service lets occur.

Time of play is crucial for team matches and this rule is just one of several that have been tried to shorten match time. The "no ad" rule was instituted to save time, as was the "eight game" set for doubles and the "ten point tiebreaker" for a third set. "No ad" didn't work as well as expected but at this writing the "eight game" set for doubles and the "ten point tiebreaker" have proved to be acceptable alternatives to traditional scoring.

The argument for playing let services is that the breaks will go both ways and there-fore the impact would be neutral. Sometimes it will give advantage to the server and some-times to the receiver. My own feeling is that the receiver will benefit slightly more. Once in a while the let will drop just over the net for a winner. More often though the let will cause the ball to pop up for an easy kill for the receiver. In singles and doubles this could be a receiver's advantage.

As the game evolves the powers that be are continually thinking of ways to make the game more enjoyable for both players and spectators. I'm all for these changes as long as they don't radically change the heart of the game. When changes are considered, the implications need to be carefully weighed.

THE BEST PLAYER OF ALL TIME – Who's your pick?

Tennis players love to debate this question. Everyone has a favorite man or woman player. Most of the time it's a champion who played during the debater's era. I don't know who first said "the older I get, the better I used to be" but this saying influences one's rational thinking about former players.

There is usually little argument that players of each current era are better and more skilled than previous players were. It wouldn't show much progress in sports or anything else if we didn't learn from our predecessors.

Athletes in virtually every sport are bound to try to exceed the records and skills of former great players. Sport, science, medicine, and technology advances of every kind demonstrate human determination to reach higher levels.

But is it necessary to compare players of yesteryear as if the playing field is level for all eras? In Phase Two I've shown how improvements in tennis courts, rackets, and strings have changed the way we play the game. The most dramatic improvement I can think of is the high speed of men's serves in today's game. Pancho Gonzales and Jack Kramer reached into the 120mph range but current players, Andy Roddick in particular, have served over 150mph. Of course, Gonzales and Kramer were using wooden rackets. Roddick uses a much higher energy graphite composite frame. For this and other reasons the playing field has changed in every era.

In my view the important thing is that players in each era stand out when they demonstrate higher skills than their contemporaries do. They produce these skills when the playing field is level for their era. They can simply do more with the same tools than their rivals can do. Therefore, they become the champions of their era.

Who's to say then, that if the old time players played on a level playing field with current champions, they couldn't be as good? All other things being equal, I think the great men and women players of any era would meet the challenges of the game.

As a player myself it's fun to talk about this and listen to other people's arguments for their choices. It's a subject that will be debated forever and there will probably never be a consensus. Maybe it's a good thing that we'll never agree, because future players then can continue to try to be the best ever!

CONCLUDING REMARKS
Concerning *WHENING* TENNIS for you

When I started this book I had no idea that it would be so much fun to write. I had a feeling that there were lots of thoughts I wanted to convey but, when I began, I couldn't know how many thoughts I had or what form the book would take.

Now I feel relieved to have set my thoughts to the written word. All the years of playing, teaching, traveling, winning, losing and all my other experiences have combined to enable me to pass these thoughts on to you.

Everyone who loves the game of tennis needs to make "when" decisions while planing, practicing, and playing the game. "In tennis as in life, TIMING is everything." As these decisions are made certain results follow. Some results will be good and some not so good. One can learn from these results in either case.

Playing tennis is fun at every level. You don't have to be "good" to enjoy playing. However, the actual process of improving one's game is also fun. Hardly anyone is adverse to improvement and, therefore, not adverse to the process either.

So listening to advice, taking lessons and reading about how to get to be a better player are all ways to improve your game. It is proven that reading is probably the hardest method of the three. Visualizing and hearing are, somehow, easier than opening a book.

I am, therefore, indebted to you for taking the time to read *WHENING* TENNIS. I also wish I could personally talk with you or demonstrate for you so it could be easier for you to get my message. Since that would be an impossible task my best way of communicating has been through this book.

I hope you have enjoyed reading it as much as I have enjoyed writing it. Let's both "keep our eye on the ball" and continue to enjoy learning and playing the great game of tennis.

Family and Friends

Yours truly hitting a forehand on a temporary grass court made in the baseball diamond at the Fig Garden Swim and Racquet Club, Fresno, California in 1969.

The under-spin, or "chip," backhand is a very versatile shot. However, top players must be able to hit over the ball for topspin when needed.

JIM REED RON LIVINGSTON COACH J D MORGAN BOB PERRY CAPT LARRY HUEBNER

NATIONAL CHAMPIONS 1953

U C L A

We had a great team at UCLA in those days. We won the NCAA Team Championship in 1952 and 1953. JD Morgan, our coach, later became the Athletic Director and really brought UCLA into national prominence.

Coach Wooden stayed with us the time he came to Fresno to speak to the Fellowship of Christian Athletes. He has had a profound influence on me, and my family. I have been truly blessed to call him a friend for over fifty years.

In 1977 we were chosen to be the "Tennis Family of the Year" in Northern California. Left to right, Jim, Gretchen, Karin, John and me.

An equally great honor for me was being inducted into the Fresno Athletic Hall of Fame in 1991. Left to right, John's wife, Kim, John, Jim's wife, Heidi, Jim, the Honoree, Gretchen, and Karin.

In 2003 we won three National Super Senior Doubles titles. Left to right, John and I won the Father/Son Clays. Karin and I won the Father/Daughter Clays, and Jim and I won the Father/Son Hardcourts. They all held me up beautifully!

"Little Bill" Johnson from San Francisco, and Ichiya Kumagae from Tokyo were two great players in the 1920's. I met "Ichy" when he was Captain of the Japanese Davis Cup team, and I was playing the grass court circuit in the 1950's.

"Big Jake" Jack Kramer dominated both the amateur and professional ranks when he played. He has also contributed greatly promoting tennis since retiring as a player.

Gene Mako made his reputation as a doubles player. However, his fitness allowed him to enter singles, doubles, and mixed doubles every time he could. Fitness and positive attitude carried him to world class heights in all events!

TONY TRABERT

My old buddy, Tony Trabert, won five Grand Slam Singles Titles and five Grand Slam Doubles Titles. He's given back so much to the game as Davis Cup Captain, and as President of the International Tennis Hall of Fame.

In 1953, at 18 years of age, Maureen Connolly became the first woman to win all four Grand Slam Singles titles. She totally dominated her era of women's tennis.

LEW HOAD

Australian Lew Hoad almost won the coveted four Grand Slam titles in 1956. After winning The Australian, French, and Wimbledon titles he lost to his buddy, Ken Rosewall in the U.S. National Championships.

" KEN ROSEWALL "

Ken Rosewall, the other Australian whiz kid, was such a great player that he was still competitive with the world's best players as a 40-year-old!

The beautiful home built by the DeVaux family in 1912 was converted to a clubhouse for the Fig Garden Swim and Racquet Club in 1963. The surrounding grounds, courts, and swimming pools have served the Fresno community well for over forty years.

GLOSSARY

"ace" – Unreturnable serve that cannot be reached by the receiver.

"around the outside" – Ball contact slightly on the side away from the player.

"back scratch" – Dropping the racket head behind one's back while serving.

"backcourt" – Area from just inside the baseline to the back fence.

"backswing" – To take racket back in preparation for forward stroke.

"ball chasing stage" – Learning period when players cannot keep the ball in play and, therefore, are constantly picking up the balls.

Challenger Circuit – Next level up from Futures Circuit tournaments.

"comfort zone" – Confident shots made by player in given situation.

"coming in shot" – Ground stroke used to approach the net.

"cross court" – Angular shot hit from one side of court to opposite side of opponent's court.

"double fault"- To miss both chances to get service into play.

"doubles chemistry" – Two players who blend well together to make a team.

"down the line" – Shot hit straight ahead along opponent's sideline.

"forecourt" – Area from service line forward to the net.

Forest Hills, New York – Former site of US National Championships. Forerunner to current US Open.

Futures Circuit – Entry level tournaments for aspiring tennis professionals.

"game" – First player to win four points, if tied at three points must win by two.

"get over" – Attempt to apply topspin to a high forehand or backhand.

"get some stick" – To hit a shot with lots of pace.

"getting in behind" – Following a shot forward to a net position.

Grand Slam Tournament – Highest level tournament in professional tennis.

"groundstroke/groundie" – Forehand or backhand drive.

"Hard court" – Tennis courts made of concrete or asphalt.

"Head Pro" – The head professional of the teaching staff.

"head speed" – Acceleration of the racket head into contact with the ball.

"heavy ball" – Shot hit with acceleration and penetration.

"hitting down" – To hit a low shot to one's opponent.

GLOSSARY, con't

"hitting zone" – Area of timely contact for racket and ball.

"hold an opponent" – To keep an opponent from moving with a well disguised shot.

"hold serve" – To win a game while serving.

"incoming server" – Player following serve to net position.

"let chord" – Ball which strikes the net band and continues over the net.

"lob" – High shot intended to drive opponent away from the net.

"match point" – The final point that, if won, ends the match.

"match" – Best two of three or three of five sets.

"miss hit" – Off center ball contact on the racket head.

NCAA – National Collegiate Athletic Association

"no no" – A shot that should not be attempted.

"not think" – To hit a shot quickly, instinctively.

NTRP – National Tennis Rating Program
"no man's land" – Area between the forecourt and backcourt.

"on the inside" – Ball contact slightly on the player's side of the ball.

"on the rise" – Hitting a groundstroke as it rises shortly after bouncing.

"overgrip" – Thin grip material that can be wrapped over standard racket grip.

"overhead/smash" – Kill shot in response to a lob.

"overplaying" – Attempting more that needed in given situation.

"passing shot/pass" – Forehand or backhand shot passing a net player for a winning point.

"poach" – Doubles tactic when player intercepts opponents return to attempt winning volley.

"point" – Starts when server places serve in proper service box. Ends with double fault, winner or error by either player.

"pronation" – Inward rolling of the wrist while serving.

"protect the lob" – Station at net which prevents a winning lob.

"punching volleys" – Very short movement toward the ball with virtually no followthrough.

"putaway volley" – Winning shot poacher makes when intercepting return.

"rainbows" – To hit shots with a high semicircle arc.

"return to center" – Balancing court in ready position for best possible coverage.

GLOSSARY, con't

"service break" – Loss of game while serving.

"service return" – Forehand or backhand used to hit service back into opponent's court.

"set" – First player to win six games, must lead by at least two games. If tied at six games each a twelve point tiebreaker must be played.

"silly bugger" – An Aussie term for a poor shot selection.

"slice serve" – Serve hit around the outside of the ball to create side spin.

"slice/chip/chop" – Shots hit with backspin/underspin.

"the T" – Intersection of the center service line with the service line.

"tie breaker" – Must be played when both players or teams have six games. In twelve point tie breaker player or team getting seven points wins if ahead by two points. If points are tied at six each, player or team must win by two points.

Title IX – Federally mandated program designed to assure gender equality in college and high school activities.

"to rally/rallying" – Players consistent exchange of shots.

"to volley/volleying" – To hit a tennis ball before it bounces.

UCLA – University of California at Los Angeles

USTA – United States Tennis Association

"volley up" – Low volley which must be hit up to clear the net.

Wimbledon – Prestigious Grand Slam tournament played on grass at the All England Club.

"winner" – Any shot that wins a point.

John Wooden – Legendary basketball coach at UCLA.

"zone/zoning" – Describes player playing above ability.

Index of Persons

Index of Persons, con't

Index of Persons, con't

Index of Places

ABOUT THE AUTHOR

Larry Huebner's life has been filled with many different tennis experiences. Few tennis book authors have experienced as large a range of tennis activities. Consequently, he has been able to write "*WHENING TENNIS*" from an uncommonly broad perspective.

His playing experiences ranged from being a U.S. Junior Davis Cup member, to Captain of his UCLA National Championship team. Later, in open play he earned a 23rd U.S. singles ranking and later still a number one U.S. singles ranking in the 45's senior division play. He has also won numerous National Father/Son, Father/Daughter championships with his children.

He has been a Head Tennis Professional and a Tennis Director and has coached beginners to National Champions, Tour, and Davis Cup players.

Knowledge of sales and purchasing of tennis equipment and clothing as well as racket stringing skills were gained as owner of a retail sporting goods store.

As a contractor, Larry put his energies into court building and club design. And he has organized and directed many local amateur and USTA professional tournaments.

Not the least of his experiences was being a tennis parent to three tennis-playing children.

He holds a Bachelor of Science degree from the University of California at Los Angeles.

ISBN 141201172-8

9 781412 011723